RITUALS *for* LIFE

For my mama and grandmothers, in honour
of their blood that flows through me, beating,
for me to remember the song of Water.

First published in Great Britain in 2022
by Laurence King Publishing
an imprint of The Orion Publishing Group Ltd
Carmelite House, 50 Victoria Embankment
London EC4Y 0DZ

An Hachette UK Company

1 3 5 7 9 10 8 6 4 2

A CIP catalogue record for this book is
available from the British Library.

ISBN 978 0 8578 2942 9

Design by Florian Michelet & Mylène Mozas
Commissioning editor: Zara Larcombe
Senior editor: Gaynor Sermon
Origination by DL Imaging Ltd, UK
Printed in China by C&C Offset Printing Co. Ltd

Laurence King Publishing is committed to ethical
and sustainable production. We are proud
participants in the Book Chain Project®.
bookchainproject.com

www.laurenceking.com
www.orionbooks.co.uk

RITUALS
for LIFE

A guide to creating meaningful rituals
inspired by nature

Isla Macleod
Illustrated by Luisa Rivera

Laurence King Publishing

An invitation, from my heart to yours

'Let the beauty of what you love be what you do.
There are hundreds of ways to kneel and kiss the ground.' – Rumi

Welcome, friend. I invite you to join me beside an ancient hearth, in this wild place where oaks grow and moss sleeps, and the dancing flames of the fire warm your weary bones. From this place, our journey begins. A journey to explore your relationship with life, revealing what is sacred to you and enriches your life with meaning and connection.

This is a journey of remembrance, of activating ancient pathways of the heart that know what it is to belong to this beautiful Earth and share in reciprocity with all life. You are never alone on this journey, and yet your way is up to you. Whichever path you choose to take, let the choice be made with clear intention from your radiant heart, inspired by your soul's yearning for wholeness.

I wish for you to unearth your most precious gifts and deepest dreams – those hidden in quiet, forgotten places because they have been forged by the darkness and strengthened in the furnace of your longing. May you tend to the wound of separation with ritual, healing that which has felt broken with the tenderest touch and intuitive crafting, to weave yourself back to oneness.

I invite you to take this leap of faith into the unknown, to say 'YES!' to life as you walk this path of the liberated heart. This path that is adorned with the beauty of intimacy and love as you spiral upon the shifting ground of birth, death and rebirth, dancing between the light and the darkness, feeling the fullness of being human.

I see the flame within you and offer this book as kindling, with bundles of inspiration to feed your inner fire so that you may shine your light courageously in the world and create an authentic spiritual life that is uniquely yours, grounded and nurtured by Nature.

Warmed beside this hearth, held within this sacred grove, get yourself comfortable, friend. Offer another log to the fire, open your eyes and ears, whisper to your heart to listen in, and let us see what wants to emerge.

Isla Macleod

Contents

Introduction

Kneeling beside my hearth, I laid out a square of tweed fabric surrounded by jars of seeds, herbs, petals and an array of symbolic objects, totems and edible foods. After I had drummed, sung and praised, calling upon the Elements to inspire and infuse this ritual, I gazed into the flames and invited my inner fire to spark life into this intention bundle and help me create a prayer that would communicate my wishes for this book, and give thanks to those energies and beings in the spirit and natural realms that would help me to birth it into the world.

After arranging the items into a visual prayer, I carefully folded the bundle and walked with it to the chestnut tree temple in my garden, resting it on the tree's roots while I dug a hole. As I placed this symbol of my prayers and intention into the damp earth, I imagined it growing roots, entwining with those of chestnut, fern and foxgloves and mingling with mycelium and wormholes. Once I had filled the hole, I bowed my head and expressed my gratitude, my love, and my wish that this book could be a gift to Nature, in some way healing the separation humans feel from the natural world and our wild, cyclical nature, so that we rediscover what is sacred and meaningful in our lives.

In this increasingly secular world, the bridges with the divine have been severed and replaced with consumerism and individualism, contributing to a global epidemic of poor mental health, inequality, collective amnesia, a crisis of meaning, and the devastating ecological situation – where up to 150 species are becoming extinct every day. How can we develop the capacity to bear witness to this without becoming overwhelmed or numb to the suffering, and make positive changes that contribute to our collective healing? How can we rediscover the sacred in the everyday and connect with forces greater than ourselves that can support and inspire us to fulfil our potential? I have found the answer to be in creating rituals for life; living intentionally and creatively, honouring our natural cycles, and collaborating with the greatest artist of all – Nature – to vision and birth a new world that is founded upon love and kindness.

At the heart of life-honouring ritual is the recognition of our relatedness and kinship with all beings and the principle of reciprocity –

the active flow of giving and receiving that ensures balance and restores right relationship between different parts of the Web of Life. It is through nurturing my relationship with nature, and exploring rituals that honour the principles of nature, that I began to heal those parts of myself that felt abandoned, rejected and powerless. The ritual life opened up the path for me to come home to the Earth and recognise my bone-deep belonging and purpose as a caretaker of life. It has provided a framework to explore the hidden, essential, wilder aspects of my soul and come into alignment with the collective wisdom of the whole. The ritual life is a journey of soul-making – a process of personal growth and psychological development that comes from creating a container to allow the forces within to be experienced consciously. By creating rituals, you learn how to open and tune your heart, body, imagination, desire and intellect to form an instrument for soulful perception that is coherent with the whole.

I discovered the benefits of ritual at an early age. Both of my parents are British but, due to my father's work, I was born in Barbados and raised in Nigeria and Japan, spending most of my education at boarding school in England. I found myself, aged eight, feeling desperately homesick in a lifeless dormitory when some flicker of inspiration or ancient memory caused me to begin a ritual practice that became a way to express my longing, create order in the chaos of my emotions and somehow feel less lonely. I would kneel before a makeshift altar, ask for help from invisible beings, ring bells to start and finish, and place food offerings in front of two Nigerian wooden figurines as I thanked them for listening.

In small ways I continued to find solace in my communication with the Mystery, addressing the pages in my journal to imagined deities and doodling strange symbols all over my workbooks.

I regularly sat in front of a Buddha that I had received for my ninth birthday, lit incense and stared at his peaceful face for hours, a part of me longing to know what he was feeling. After the trials of early adulthood left me lost and depressed in a material world where I could find no meaning, I made my way to a Buddhist meditation retreat in my twenties, searching for answers. My soul ached for the wild unknown, for forgotten realms, and for a relationship with the sacred in a way that I couldn't articulate but that I felt every time I stared at my smiling Buddha.

By good grace, the fire of my soul was stoked through my experiences and encounters while on retreat. I saw the world with new eyes, recognising the connection between all beings and the extraordinary gift of life I had been given. One starry night, I devoted myself to a life of spiritual service on a hilltop overlooking the River Dart as I vowed to heal the bridges to the divine and in some way *become the bridge*. Without a template of how this could look, I listened to the call of the wild and the longing to find my place in the natural world, and ventured to live alone in an ancient woodland in Sussex. I made my home in a yurt, living alongside ash, hazel, oak and holly, beside a wildflower meadow that was a hunting ground to a majestic barn owl. I became an apprentice to Nature, a disciple of the trees, following the rhythms of the Sun and Moon as I refined my ritual craft as a path of healing separation.

I offer this book as a guide to support you in creating your own bridges back to nature and the divine, so you can cultivate a resonant spiritual life that is uniquely yours, that honours the sacred however it manifests for you in your everyday life. This connection feeds your sense of inner resource and wellbeing as you recognise the many ways you are supported, and the natural intelligence and sacredness of your body. Through crafting rituals you create the space to be present with your inner experience, explore and express your emotions and integrate the ongoing changes of your life in an embodied and intentional way. You can experience the beauty of your creativity, the fullness of your power, the depth of your belonging, and develop the capacity to hold space for yourself and others through life's ups and downs. You will also hone the skills of intention-setting, clear communication, and imaginative visioning and prime your senses to appreciate the more subtle energetic realms.

We each have a unique gift to bring to the world, but we also share a communal story that informs our perception and experience of life. What I believe is being asked of us at this pivotal time is a spiritual revolution that shifts our current systems and ways of seeing the world towards the reality of oneness – that *we are all related.* The ritual life is a revolutionary path that can awaken our consciousness to the inherent sacredness of all life and re-enchant the world with wonder and new possibilities. By acknowledging the exquisite diversity of the whole, the different dimensions of existence, and by reinstating the feminine principle – the creative force that embraces inclusivity and the wisdom of the cycles – we can expand our perception of what it means to be human, in relationship with all life.

Instead of striving to fix the *symptoms* of ecological breakdown, human division and disease, we must look to the root cause of the disconnection that has allowed the current situation to arise. Making this transition requires us to cultivate the collective imagination so that we can go beyond adapting to the present systems, and actually reshape and create the future we want to inhabit. Providing a space to engage the active imagination through creativity and visualisation, ritual is a playground for you to explore your dreams and ideas and put you in touch with your life force and the seeds of potential within that already know how to create a more beautiful, thriving and harmonious world.

As the gardener of your soul, it is up to you to find the tools that will help you weed out what is binding you and cultivate practices that enable the seeds of your longing to bear fruit. For the most part, the rituals I offer in this book are intended to support your journey of soul-making and the cultivation of a personal ritual practice. All the rituals are designed to enrich your understanding of your natural cycles and re-enchant your relationship with nature, offering a combination of tools, invitations and frameworks that are as relevant to urban dwellers as they are to rural homesteaders. I also include several community rituals that are intended to revive the sacredness in more common transitional rites such as naming days and funerals.

As your guide on this journey, my intention is to provide

a strong foundation from which your ritual life can evolve in its own unique way.

Part I of the book explores the purpose and potential of ritual, fostering an understanding of how incorporating it into your life can support and inspire you to live more intentionally, intimately and creatively. I share key concepts found within indigenous wisdom across cultures, which can be cultivated within a ritual life to restore connection, relatedness and an appreciation of the sacred.

Part II is devoted to preparing the ground for your ritual life, with tools and suggestions of how to create an effective and balanced ritual, including energetic clearing, opening and closing sacred space, and making an invocation. Once a strong ritual container is established, you are ready to bring the ritual to life with the Four Seeds (intention, creativity, gratitude and kindness) that I have experienced as guiding forces inherent in life-giving, nature-inspired rituals. The Four Seeds provide a simple framework for creating authentic, bespoke rituals, and carry within them the potential to enrich your everyday experience when they are repeatedly sown as part of your ritual life. I offer some playful invitations of how to cultivate these seeds that will deepen your understanding of their intrinsic energies and how they relate to the seasons.

Part III, the main section of the book, contains 20 practical rituals arranged into the four seasons. I guide you on a journey through spring, summer, autumn and winter to show how the energetic qualities of each season relate to the four Elements of Air, Fire, Water and Earth and reflect your own natural transitions and growth cycles. Guided by the intelligence of Nature, you can craft your rituals in ways that honour these seasonal energies to support the manifestation of the outcome you desire. I suggest simple daily rituals to help connect you with the seasonal energies and corresponding Elements, before laying out five detailed rituals for each season that you can create to honour your natural transitions.

Through your ritual craft you can celebrate all aspects of being human and cultivate a heart-centred way of responding to change and the unknown. When you feel lost, anxious, alone and cut off from your vital life force and potential, a ritual will help you recalibrate, enabling you to make peace with the past and direct your internal compass for the way forward. It feels vital to bring a fresh perspective to the function of ritual so you can choose how you wish to mark and honour the transitions and significant moments in your life in meaningful ways. Through your recognition and celebration of these moments, you weave your life with intention and become aware of the transformative energies at play that you can collaborate with. The ritual life invites you to re-enchant your sense of the sacred, so that you recognise the spiritual dimension within all your transitions, relationships and actions and your innate capacity to create the world you long for.

Note on the use of language

In writing this book, I am aware that words such as sacred, divine, holy and blessing carry religious connotations that may be divisive. I have found deep healing can come from the reclamation of spiritual language in service to re-enchanting the world, healing the rift between the physical and invisible realms. I invite you to feel into what words resonate with you, so you can communicate with the sacred in an authentic way in ritual space.

With regard to the language around gender: to acknowledge the animacy of nature, I tend towards referring to all beings from the natural world as 'she', 'he' or 'them', based on my experience of their feminine and masculine energetic aspects and inherited models of gender, but I recognise this interpretation is based upon ancient definitions of difference that are now becoming challenged with the truth of gender fluidity. This book is written for all genders, human and more-than-human, and the seeds of life that are yet to be born.

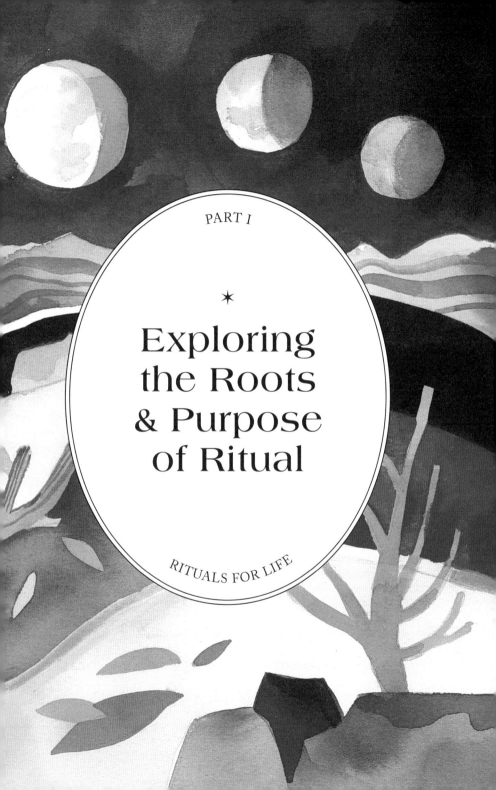

PART I

✳

Exploring the Roots & Purpose of Ritual

RITUALS FOR LIFE

The Essence of Ritual:
What Do We Mean by It
and What Does It Involve?

'The purpose of ritual is to connect us to our own essence, to help
us tune into the collective spirit, or to mend whatever is broken,
whatever wires have been pulled out of one's life, so we can start
anew. Ritual is to the soul what food is to the physical body.'
– Sobonfu Somé: healer, the Dagara people of Burkina Faso

We will begin by exploring what ritual entails so that you understand
the broader context within which the rituals in this book sit. The word
'ritual' conjures different images depending on your cultural upbring-
ing and personal history, so it is helpful to reimagine what ritual
means for *you*. This first section offers my interpretations, but as your
ritual path unfolds you will begin to know what ritual is through the
wisdom of your experience, and that is the only real truth.

In this book, ritual refers to intentional, symbolic actions that
create balance and connection – within ourselves, with the Earth
community, the powerful rhythms of the Cosmos and the invisible
dimensions of spirit. Through these symbolic actions you convey
messages to your psyche, or soul, that act like spiritual keys, revealing
a deeper truth about who and what you are in relation to the whole.

For consistency, this interpretation of ritual includes ceremonies, rites and celebrations, recognising their shared function to
communicate with the sacred, enhance connection and honour
life transitions. Some of the modern rituals you are probably
familiar with are:

- BIRTHDAYS
- WEDDINGS
- NAMING CEREMONIES, BAPTISMS
  AND CHRISTENINGS
- FUNERALS
- ANNIVERSARIES AND MEMORIALS
- OPENING CEREMONIES
  FOR SPORTING EVENTS
- CORONATIONS AND
  INAUGURATIONS
- GRADUATIONS
- HOUSEWARMING PARTIES
- HEN AND STAG (BACHELORETTE/
  BACHELOR) PARTIES
- BAR/BAT MITZVAHS
- SEASONAL FESTIVALS

Honouring transitions –
a container for transformation

Most of these more well-known rituals acknowledge a rite of passage, since it is through a ritual process that you can cultivate wholeness after an evolution has occurred. This is one of the most important functions of ritual – to honour a time of transition – as it helps us to navigate change and midwife our own transformation. Whether you are celebrating a transition into married life, welcoming a child into a family or marking the end of a relationship or way of life, the invitation of ritual is to create the space to meet yourself and your process so that you can accept and integrate the changes.

Storytelling

There is a structure inherent in ritual that reflects the form of any narrative that has a beginning, middle and end and follows the three stages of a rite of passage, starting with:

1) **Separation**, as you leave behind everyday life and cross the threshold into ritual space where you then undergo 2) a **transition** or transformation, before you 3) **return** and integrate your experience. Since ritual is a form of storytelling, a mythopoetic journey that conveys symbols, it follows that this structure is needed to create balance and wholeness. In this book I offer the Four Seeds (see page 58) as a complementary framework that can help you connect with the regenerative, cyclical energies of nature and the potential of activating these seeds and incorporating them into your everyday life.

Soul-making

The structural components of ritual are woven together with your own artistry and the unique symbols that speak to your soul, creating a sacred experience and journey of remembering. This is about soul-making – the expression and integration of the Jungian notion of the shadow-self and your innate gifts, married with attending to the river of your longing – the current that stirs your deepest dreams and desires – and listening to the wisdom of your heart.[1] Crafting ritual also requires you to reinstate your imagination as your guide and inspiration as you traverse invisible realms, explore your subconscious, and vision the beautiful, enchanted, harmonious world that, deep down, you know is possible.

Communicating with the sacred

Living a ritual life will cultivate the pathways of belonging, wholeness and meaning from your willingness to invite the Creator, gods, goddesses, the sacred, divinity, or higher power into your midst and communicate with them in a way that is authentic for you. Nurturing this relationship is the key to crafting effective ritual, requiring you to find the spiritual language and symbols that resonate to enable this conversation with the sacred to reverberate meaningfully.

Cultivating connection and meaning

Rituals are essentially a vehicle for relatedness, facilitating the fundamental human need for connection with the sacred, purpose, a sense of identity and the wider Earth community. Creating rituals can help you to experience the world as a living, evolving communion of subjects with a common origin story and shared destiny. As you expand your perception of the multi-dimensionality of life through your rituals, you will become attuned to the subtler energies weaving everything together.

A tool for remembering

Creating a ritual helps to awaken your innate wisdom as an indigenous person who belongs to the Earth, whose purpose is caring for and attending to life. Even though many in the modern, secular world feel little or no connection with their indigenous past, we all come from the seeds of our ancestors' prayers and carry the blueprint of how to live in harmony with the natural world.

A ritual life will support you in cultivating presence, deep listening and trust in the unknown so that you feel the confidence to follow your intuition and create rituals that come from deep within you. You will begin to remember the ways in which your ancestors honoured the sacred, while responding to the moment with curiosity and the willingness to explore what arises in the context of your life here and now.

The Potential of Ritual:
Why Do We Need It and
How Can We Benefit From It?

*'Action on behalf of life transforms. Because the relationship
between self and the world is reciprocal, it is not a question
of first getting enlightened or saved and then acting.
As we work to heal the Earth, the Earth heals us.'*
– Robin Wall Kimmerer: Director of the Center for Native
Peoples and the Environment, State University of New York

I have experienced so many benefits from living a ritual life, and the
seeds of intention I have sown through my rituals continue to grow and
bear fruit. By exploring the potential of ritual in this section I will reveal
some of the ways in which ritual can empower you and enrich your life,
and the lives of others, by meeting individual and collective needs.

Expands perception of the spiritual dimensions of life

When you create ritual, your personal identification becomes intimately
woven with the world around you, the invisible realms, the Elements,
and the Cosmos. Your awareness and identity grow beyond the confines
of your physical body and become part of a collective whole. Through
the process of co-creating with the invisible forces, you become attuned
to the constant dance of creation and those subtler realms of energy
that physicists, shamans and mystics know so well. This realisation of
oneness is one of the greatest gifts of ritual.

Re-enchants the world

When you are turned on to the reality of oneness, the paradigm of
separation and individualism starts to come apart at the seams and
a world of potential opens up. As you serenade the sacred through
ritual, you experience your own sacredness through the intimacy of
this union and the world becomes re-enchanted with wonder, beauty
and everyday miracles. You become tuned into the frequency of love
and the attendant qualities of kindness, compassion and generosity.
Your life becomes an offering of gratitude for Creation.

Personal empowerment

Living a ritual life enables you to actively participate in the conscious evolution of the Earth, seeding the possibility of a reciprocal and regenerative culture. By choosing the path of ritual you restore agency to your life, choosing where to direct your energy and what you want to participate in, as well as creating an authentic spiritual practice that honours what you hold sacred.

As you dance with the sacred, you can direct your life in a more intentional and meaningful way, make friends with change, and feel a sense of control amid the chaos. Ritual provides an active form of self-care that hones your ability to cultivate inner trust and authority so you can listen to your authentic self and not be governed by external forces.

Healing and integration

Ritual functions as a bridge between the seen and unseen, conscious and unconscious, known and unknown, that can be traversed by creating the space to meet yourself exactly where you are and focusing your intention on which way you want to go. By taking responsibility for your life using a metaphoric process you will learn the language of your unconscious so you can heal and integrate challenging emotions, rather than allowing them to govern your life in unhelpful ways.

This inquiry into the self helps bring your inner and outer worlds into congruence so you can live a more liberated existence, while revealing your true nature as an active participant and conscious co-creator within the Web of Life (see page 21). This radically shifts the apex of power in our modern world back to nature and that which is inherent in you that *is* nature.

Alignment with nature

Creating rituals for yourself and your community enables you to align with the powers and intelligence of Nature and the Cosmos directly. By honouring your natural life cycles through ritual, you come into harmony with the rhythms of the natural world, learning to accept the inevitability of death, how to die well, and welcoming death as an opportunity for rebirth and renewal. In recognising Nature's intelligence, the feminine principle is brought back online to create balance, and the systems of oppression that have denied the wisdom of the body, of the darkness and of nature unravel, reinstating the value of feeling and the imaginal, primal and unconscious realms of the soul.[2] By attending to the web of relations that make up the living world through ritual, you are healing the perceived chasm between the material and spiritual worlds and strengthening the web of relationships you are a part of, cultivating connection and fostering a deep and unshakeable sense of belonging.

There are many benefits to creating rituals, more than I can explore here, but below is a brief summary of some of the gifts that ritual can bring to your life:

BENEFITS OF RITUAL

- Teaches how to live more intentionally
- Nurtures creativity
- Expands awareness of the sacred
- Cultivates a sense of wholeness and belonging
- Deepens trust and acceptance of natural life cycles, supporting you through life's transitions
- Exercises intuition and deep listening skills
- Restores connection with nature, the self and others
- Helps process challenging emotions
- Cultivates intimate, reciprocal and conscious relationships
- Nurtures a sense of purpose and meaningful life
- Restores balance within the Web of Life
- Dismantles external power structures and restores power within, revealing inner wisdom
- Strengthens concentration, ability to focus and presence

The Roots of Ritual:
Ancient Wisdom for Modern Times

'Most native societies around the world had three common characteristics: they had an intimate, conscious relationship with their place; they were stable 'sustainable' cultures, often lasting for thousands of years; and they had a rich ceremonial and ritual life. They saw these three as intimately connected.'

– Dolores LaChapelle: environmental philosopher and scholar

There is a great deal you can learn, or remember, by exploring the ancient wisdom of Indigenous peoples who recognise the sacred and spiritual dimensions of life. The path of ritual has been well-trodden in human history, and there are many breadcrumbs to follow. Enriching your understanding with some of the shared beliefs that form the basis of Indigenous cultures expands your perception of reality and reinforces the purpose of rituals to honour and bless life and express a deeper level of communion with the natural world. I outline some of this wisdom here for you to reflect upon, and invite you to consider how these ways of seeing the world can inspire your ritual life.

'We are all related'

Indigenous cultures that have upheld the principles of nature, living in intimate and conscious relationship with the places they inhabit, carry the seeds of potential within all of us that speak of the interrelatedness of life on Earth. When a native elder speaks of treating nature with reverence, there is the belief that what you do to the land, you do to yourself.

In the Lakota language of one of the Native American Sioux tribes there is no word for 'animal' because all creatures are part of the same family. This is epitomised by the phrase *Mitákuye Oyás'iŋ*, meaning 'we are all related'. Similarly, in the Native American Cree dialect there is no word for 'isolation' – the concept of separation does not exist. It is this perception that prevails in shamanic and animist belief systems that are rooted in the cellular knowledge of the aliveness and sentience of all life and the inclusion of all beings as kin.

The Web of Life

This is the energy matrix of all existence that connects all life and recognises the world as an animate and integrated whole. Living as a part of this web, every thought, feeling and action ripples outward and will vibrate back in some form. Most Indigenous societies have a rich ceremonial life because they appreciate this principle of nature and the responsibility we have as humans to attend to the web with intention and care. They understand how to look beneath the surface of things and tap into the powerful natural forces that dwell there, accessing streams of energy to gain vitality and inspiration in their lives.

The importance placed on honouring life transitions with rites of passage and initiation rituals in Indigenous cultures demonstrates their awareness of how the human journey is inextricably linked with the evolving energies of Nature and the Cosmos, and the value of ritual in integrating these changes.

Holistic view of health

Indigenous peoples the world over honour their relationship with the natural and more-than-human worlds because they understand that their lives depend on this relationship.[3] Living more intimately with nature, they know the effects their actions have on the world around them and recognise the way this affects their own wellbeing and the beating heart of the tribe.

Any illness or crisis that affects tribal life is seen as an expression of energetic imbalance and the role of the shaman or medicine man/woman is to act as mediator between worlds to restore harmony and the natural flow of energy through practices such as ritual, prayer, offerings and with the help of plant spirits. This holistic view of health considers the complex web of relationships that affect humans on every level, not just the physical. From the Indigenous perspective, something cannot be understood until it is known by all four aspects of the human being: mind, body, emotions and spirit, respecting the different components of experience that together bring about wholeness.

UPPER WORLD

CELESTIAL REALM

SPIRIT GUIDES,
ALLIES AND ANGELS

DIVINATION

FUTURE

MIDDLE WORLD

PHYSICAL REALM

HUMANS, ANIMALS
AND PLANTS

EMBODIMENT

PRESENT

LOWER WORLD

SHADOW REALM

ANCESTORS AND
POWER ANIMALS

TRANSFORMATION

PAST

The Tree of Life

One way of depicting this reality is demonstrated by the symbol of the Tree of Life, or World Tree in shamanic traditions.[4] The Tree of Life reveals the different dimensions of reality that coexist and collaborate through a vertical dimension, the *Axis Mundi*.[5] This is the central axis that runs through the worlds, which shamans use to travel between dimensions and create a bridge between the physical and spiritual realms. The middle world is represented by the trunk, symbolising the physical reality we inhabit that connects us with the other worlds; the lower world is depicted as being the roots, or underworld, where our ancestors can be found; the upper spirit world can be reached by the branches of the Tree of Life. If the invisible realms are not acknowledged and attended to by those in the middle world, imbalance occurs and the tree is cut off from its roots and unable to bear fruit.

Honouring ancestors

In many Indigenous cultures the veneration of ancestors is a vital part of community life, honouring those who birthed us and seeded their dreams, wisdom and resilience within us. In the Yoruba tradition (an ethnic group native to western Africa), the dead are buried at home and not in a cemetery so that the family can wish their ancestors good morning each day and good night before they go to bed. When someone dies a loved one says '*Odabo*', which means 'see you soon', because the ancestors will visit in dreams or visions and be attended to in daily life with prayers and offerings at an ancestral shrine.

Festivals dedicated to tending the spirits of the dead are present worldwide in the Celtic Samhain, Mexican Day of the Dead, and Obon in Japan, creating a vital, rich landscape of belonging. By ritually attending the dead, the living create a bridge to the invisible realms, helping the dead to cross over and become healthy ancestors who can help guide and inspire the living. An awareness of their presence and influence can also help the living disentangle from inherited beliefs and patterns that have been passed down.

The Children's Fire

Another way people's lives have been guided is by those yet to be born that will inherit this Earth. Indigenous Native American chiefs looked to the wisdom of nature, the circle of natural law, when they constructed their councils. They saw the need for balance between the feminine and masculine in creation, so they ensured both men and women had a voice in their councils.

They also recognised that all beings of nature give primacy to the love of their children, and so 'as they constructed the councils within which laws were made, placed a small fire in the middle of the council circle which they called the Children's Fire ... a pledge of the chiefs, a promise to themselves – no law, no decision, no action emerging from this council shall be allowed that in any way will harm the children now or forever.'[6] This includes the offspring of the animal and plant realms too. With the Children's Fire at the centre of their decision-making, these councils ensured their actions would be in harmony with natural laws and support a flourishing future for life on Earth.

Original Instructions

Indigenous peoples have acted as guardians of life, dedicated to nurturing their relationships and living in harmony with the natural world so that they fulfil their responsibility as human beings to be caretakers of the Earth. The Kogi people of the Sierra Nevada de Santa Marta in Colombia believe that their entire mountain range is an integrated living totality, part of the Great Mother's body, and globally the world's heart. They live according to her Original Instructions – that all creation must be protected and nurtured. The Kogi believe they exist to care for the world and maintain the equilibrium of life through their rituals, offerings, songs and prayers, which are carried out along a network of interconnected sacred sites.

For many of America's Indigenous peoples the Original Instructions provide a clear purpose for the role of humans on Earth. They speak to living in gratitude and kinship, with a reverence for community and creation. Put simply, they say that we are supposed to live 'in a good way'.

The indigenous spirit

If you trace your ancestry back far enough, you will discover you have Earth-honouring ancestors who lived in harmony with the natural world, lived by the cycles of the Sun and the Moon, and honoured the invisible spirits that were as much a part of life as the visible world. You carry this blueprint – their DNA, their memories, their prayers and dreams. Their wild, native spirit lives on in you, and will guide you home to the Earth.

It is vital at this time that you remember your indigenous spirit and your belonging to this Earth. This ancient knowledge is threatened by modern science-based thought that values the rational and logical, denying the essential role of the sacred, invisible and mysterious. It is crucial for the future of life on Earth that we respect and remember indigenous wisdom. By creating rituals for life you can actively clear the pathways that connect you with these ancient ways of knowing and help revive the modes of perception that cultivate kinship, reciprocity and kindness.

The Gifts of Nature: You Don't Need to Go Out Into Nature. You *Are* Nature.

'One touch of nature makes the whole world kin.'
– William Shakespeare, *Troilus and Cressida*, Act III, Scene iii

The natural world is my greatest source of inspiration for living a ritual life. The rituals in this book are designed to connect you with the fundamental building blocks of nature – the Elements – and honour your natural cycles so that you can cultivate the pathways of memory that reveal *you are an expression of nature.*

Embedded in our current systems are so many limiting beliefs about how we perceive and about what nature is that you need to go into the world on your own, abandoning your preconceptions, so that your wild edges are given space to feel again, and the more subtle and multi-dimensional realms come into focus. Allowing your senses to be restored to receivers of communication that are collaborating with the Earth's sensory body helps to dissolve illusory boundaries so that you can enter into dialogue with the natural world and experience participatory consciousness – the merging and identification with your surroundings.

This section is devoted to expanding on the gifts of Nature as teacher, healer and artist, and the ways the natural world can inspire your rituals, starting with a summary of the principles that can guide you towards living in harmonious relationship with all life.

THE PRINCIPLES OF NATURE

The Web of Life – all life is connected, sacred and bound by cause and effect

Life cycles – everything changes through the transformative process of birth, decay, death and rebirth

Reciprocity – balance is preserved by a harmonious flow of giving and receiving

The Elements – reflect the simplest essential properties and principles of all worldly matter, making life on Earth possible

Adaptation – follow the path of least resistance

No waste – everything is valuable and must go somewhere

Teacher

These principles are some of the fundamental teachings of Nature that you can witness in action everywhere. When you acknowledge them, you turn on your innate intelligence that knows how to live in accordance with these principles. You can make sense of the changes in your life and the natural ebb and flow of beginnings and endings, embracing the opportunity for renewal and transformation.

The natural world shows you how to embody regenerating rhythms by letting go of what is no longer serving you, giving yourself space for fallow time, to compost, integrate and gather your energy for outward growth and creativity. This invitation is inherent within every circle of the Sun and Moon and the menstruation cycle of women, calling for you to embrace your wild, flowing nature.

As you learn to translate the language of nature, there is more than mere astonishment at what you might uncover: the knowledge of what trees feel and how they communicate; of how other animal consciousnesses experience the world; of mini ecosystems such as lichen – a composite organism of fungi and algae that grows from a process of fusion, challenging some of our basic assumptions about life. Like any remarkable teacher, Nature inspires a sense of wonder and curiosity, leading you to inquire deeper into the mystery and expand your sense of what's possible.

Trees have been some of my greatest teachers; embodying the rhythm of the seasons so gracefully, expressing themselves so whole-heartedly, deeply rooted, resilient, adaptable, and masters of patience and perseverance. Using the native British lunar calendar, I have spent years working with the thirteen sacred trees that are connected with each cycle of the Moon, creating rituals to communicate with the spirits of the different trees and learn from their wisdom and healing medicine.[7] I also turned towards other elders of the natural world: nettle, mugwort, rose, heather, rosemary, stone, water and fungi; each one revealing more of the Mystery and the potential of cultivating an intimate relationship with the more-than-human worlds.

Through nature's intrinsic intelligence and physical expression, we are shown how to live in a community, self-organise, care for our young, respect our elders, defend ourselves, play, adapt to change and respect the power and wisdom of the darkness – the fertile void where life begins within each seed. Nature speaks of deep time kept by mountains, ice and rock that demands humility from us humans who are so governed by time, but only for our short lives. Nature's way is wild and playful, inviting us to lay down our cloak of civility and dance naked under the Moon.

Healer

You are healed by nature through the ongoing invitation to come into conscious relationship through your body and senses, honouring the ways you are made up of the Elements, an expression of nature's principles.

If you live in an urban setting, seemingly removed from the natural world, you are still intimately woven with the forces of nature, composed of the same Elements, a carrier of life. Your bones and flesh are made of Earth, your blood flows with Water, carrying ancient memories within. With every breath you take you drink in the Air, in duet with the trees and oceans, connecting you with all other beings. Your body is warmed and awakened to life by the Fire that moves through you, calling you to create and express yourself in the world. The Elements are your keys to communion, the shamans of the natural world who provide the bridge to the more-than-human realms. You don't need to *go out into* nature. You *are* nature.

In reconnecting your physical body to nature, your innate healing capacity is switched on. Instead of relying on pharmaceuticals, you can choose to work with healing plants and create a synergy with the natural world. Humans have been collaborating with plants in this way for millennia, appealing to the spirits of trees, fungi, herbs and flowers to share their medicine and restore balance. Life is dependent on the sustenance the living Earth provides and ingesting wild and homegrown food connects you with the creative force inherent in nature. You are what you eat, and all the intelligence imbued in each seed, the power of the Elements and the generosity of the human and more-than-human beings who helped grow your food are present in each mouthful.

Homeopathy, herbalism, flower remedies, Ayurvedic and Chinese medicine all recognise the healing power of nature, and modern research is beginning to catch up. Recent studies reveal the extent to which humans benefit physically, cognitively, socially, emotionally and spiritually from spending time in nature. From reducing stress, depression, anxiety, ADD symptoms, crime rates and aggression to improving mood, boosting immunity, promoting calm and increasing self-esteem, there are so many ways the natural world can nurture feelings of well-being and togetherness.[8] The resurgence in pilgrimage and the growth of forest schools, ecopsychology and *shinrin-yoku*, or 'forest-bathing', point towards a desperate yearning for more immersive interaction with the natural world and also highlight the danger of nature being commodified – that we need to pay, subscribe or be guided to experience the natural world. There is no doubt a value in learning from others, but it is through *you* defining your relationship with Gaia that will imbue it with life and soul and love.[9]

Artist

As a consummate artist, Nature demonstrates the sublime potential of creativity, bestowing magnificent beauty and colour on the world. Each snowflake, leaf, feather, seed, flower and crystal came into being as a gesture of love, through the sacred union of opposites. The creative intelligence that imbues all life starts as a seed in the imagination that is birthed from your willingness to collaborate with the unknown, and playfully, tenderly open yourself to new possibilities.

This marriage between soul and nature liberates your imagination and radically transforms your perception of who and what you are. When you hear the song of the nightingale echoing through the moonlit night and know it as a voice of yours or feel your skin dissolve as you submerge in the sea, you have come undone, and the silent truth of your being is what remains.

Courting the Earth through ritual takes you to realms beyond words, where *you* become the message, your life an expression of your love. It reminds you that you are in relationship with the natural world and the evolution of the planet, a valuable part of creation, woven together with something wildly mysterious and undefinable. The ritual life honours your innate creativity and power to transform and birth new life by inviting the artist within to express the exquisite beauty of your soul. It shows you how to communicate from your heart with your body, words and actions, and sing your joy with reverence. When you open to receive the gifts of nature you dissolve the edges that keep you apart and heal those places in you that feel unworthy, abandoned, ashamed and alone as you embrace what is your birthright – your belonging to this Earth.

Sources of Ritual Inspiration: The Five Branches

'The world is but a canvas to our imagination'
– Henry David Thoreau, naturalist and philosopher

The path of ritual has its genesis in the journey of the soul and the human longing to find meaning in life. Depending on your own experiences, you will gravitate towards different sources of inspiration to carve out what meaning you imbue your life with, and what rituals you feel excited to create. From my own journey I have found five strands of inspiration with their source in the natural world that can give your rituals purpose. I include them here as a reference to support you in creating a ritual life beyond exploring those I share in Part III.

I refer to these as the Five Branches, since they grow from the Tree of Remembrance that reminds us of the wealth of ancestral and shared memory that goes deep into the roots of the Earth, connecting us with primordial, instinctive ways of knowing.

THE FIVE BRANCHES

- LIFE CYCLES
- THE WHEEL OF THE YEAR
- THE ELEMENTS
- SYMBOLS, MYTH AND ARCHETYPES
- ANCESTORS

These branches can grow in any direction and will be expressed differently according to your unique style and intention. They will become adorned with leaves, blooms and fruit as you give life to them through ritual. While the Five Branches provide the inspiration for the rituals in this book, symbols, myth and archetypes are explored most effectively as part of your personal practice, since your soul will resonate with specific images and stories, and deeper healing and integration can occur when you learn the language of your soul. It is beyond the scope of this book to provide extensive examples of symbols, myths and archetypes, but helpful books are included in the resources.

You can refer to the Five Branches when you are considering the intention of any ritual you want to create, listening to what feels most alive in you and is ripe for harvesting.

Life cycles

In a world where the only constant is change, there is a need to mark significant transitions by creating ritual space. In this ritual cocoon, the deeper currents that swell in you can rise to the surface, revealing what is seeking to be born and nurtured for this next phase of growth.

Rites of passage have always been a feature of human life, since birth and death are the thresholds we cross as we arrive and leave this world, but there are many more experiences of 'births' and 'deaths' throughout our lives that provide opportunities for recalibration. Supporting others to honour their transitions is a fundamental part of my work as a ritualist, providing a sacred space for people to mark significant changes in their life. Creating ritual to let go of a relationship, job, limiting belief or phase of your life can help you to release on an energetic and psychological level and cultivate greater acceptance and forgiveness of what is hard to bear. It is equally important to honour new beginnings and projects, activating them with your clear intention and vision for the future.

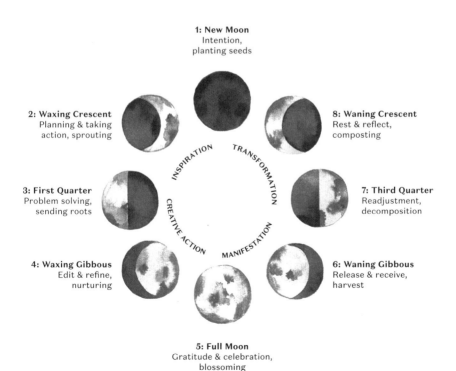

1: New Moon
Intention,
planting seeds

2: Waxing Crescent
Planning & taking
action, sprouting

8: Waning Crescent
Rest & reflect,
composting

INSPIRATION   TRANSFORMATION

3: First Quarter
Problem solving,
sending roots

7: Third Quarter
Readjustment,
decomposition

CREATIVE ACTION   MANIFESTATION

4: Waxing Gibbous
Edit & refine,
nurturing

6: Waning Gibbous
Release & receive,
harvest

5: Full Moon
Gratitude & celebration,
blossoming

The natural cycles of the stars, Sun, Moon and planets reflect your own inner motions and the phases you go through. The rituals in this book are crafted around the seasons, but all natural cycles reflect these phases of birth, growth, decay, death and rebirth. As the Moon pulls at your tides each month, you experience your own internal rhythms and are energetically supported to go through a life cycle. From the quiet beginnings of the new moon to the bright abundance of the full moon, you experience four phases of intention-setting, gathering feedback, making adjustments and celebrating your harvest. As the Moon's light fades from full moon to the dark moon, you experience the waning phase of the cycle: exploring your gratitude, letting go, and going within to reflect and digest.

I often create rituals with the phases of the Moon as a way of aligning with the natural energies most present to support me in consciously creating my life. I write down my intentions for the month on the new moon and add these to my altar. I hold a Fire ritual on the full moon to reflect and give thanks for the flourishing of my intention and let go of anything I feel has hindered my growth by writing them on a piece of paper and offering it to the fire along with some herbs to feed the flames.

Connecting with the rhythms of the Moon, the menstrual cycle, the movement of the stars, planets and Sun, and the phases of human development – from childhood to puberty, adulthood and elderhood – by creating rituals to mark significant thresholds, you can enrich your appreciation of the impermanence of life. Aligning with nature's principles you innately know when to be actively creating, expressive and expansive, and when to be receptive, to rest and reflect to support a regenerative and sustainable way of living.

The Wheel of the Year

This seasonal map from the Celtic tradition offers eight energetic gateways to commune with and celebrate the transitions in nature so that you intentionally cross the threshold to another phase of your journey in harmony with the natural forces. They provide an outline for creating a ritual life that celebrates the wisdom of nature. The Wheel of the Year is marked by the four fixed quarter points – winter/summer solstice and spring/autumn equinox – and the cross-quarter points – Samhain, Imbolc, Beltane and Lammas – also known as the great fire festivals.

In the northern hemisphere, the eight festivals are celebrated across these thresholds:

Samhain – end October/beginning November
Winter solstice – 20th–23rd December
Imbolc – end January/beginning February
Spring equinox – 20th–23rd March
Beltane – end April/beginning May
Summer solstice – 20th–23rd June
Lammas – end July/beginning August
Autumn equinox – 20th–23rd September

In the southern hemisphere, these dates can be advanced six months so as to coincide with the natural seasons as they occur in the local climates. When a community is celebrating Samhain in Scotland, a family in Australia will be marking Beltane, for instance. The festivals are positioned around the wheel in the direction they are energetically associated with; for example, the spring equinox is in the east as the place of the rising sun and new beginnings, as the natural world is born again after the darkness of winter. The directions also correspond with the Element that is most present at that seasonal shift, with the energy of Air prevailing over the east, as you open to receive inspiration and give voice to your intention that will guide your growth over the coming year.

You can create rituals to honour these festivals to anchor you for a moment in this constantly changing world, to pause, reflect, give thanks and seed your intention for the next cycle of growth. Each festival has a distinctive flavour and focus, with associations to different gods and goddesses, trees and myths. In the Celtic tradition the triple fire goddess Brighid is, for example, honoured at Imbolc as she breathes life into the mouth of dead winter, tapping the earth with her birch wand to quicken the life lying dormant and activate the seeds sleeping in the soil. As guardian of the hearth of the home, I have included Brighid in the home-warming ritual in the spring rituals section of Part III for you to acquaint yourself with her, if you haven't already!

As well as ancient rites that continue to be celebrated, such as the union of the masculine and feminine energies in the Beltane maypole dance, you can create your own seasonal rituals to align with the energies of nature and awaken their potential within you. Whether alone or with your family or community, these festivals can enrich your sense of belonging and understanding of the principles of nature and the energies present through the seasonal changes that can support your full flourishing.

The Elements

The sacred Elements of Earth, Air, Fire and Water are the essential components that make up all worldly matter. Energetically connected with the seasons of the Wheel of the Year, the Elements categorise the material world into four parts (five if you include Spirit or Essence in the centre) and provide the bridge that connects you to your true nature. It is important to include symbolic representations of the Elements in your ritual, such as a stone, feather, candle or a bowl of water, so their energies are activated and balanced to support the creative process of manifestation. I have a portable ritual bundle that includes a symbol of each of the Elements so that I can easily create an effective ritual wherever I am.

You can also create rituals to invoke specific Elements if you want to strengthen their qualities in your life. Expanding your understanding of the inherent powers of each Element and the ways they work within you helps you to see when things are not in equilibrium and require adjustment. For example, when you are preoccupied in thought, flitting from one thing to another, your Air Element needs to be balanced with the grounding of Earth, so you can create a ritual that incorporates holding a stone, walking barefoot or sitting with your back against a tree as you imagine your roots reaching deep into the soil.

As well as their physical aspects, each Element has metaphoric associations connected with their corresponding season. For example, connected with autumn in the west is Water, guardian of the mysteries of the emotional realms, dreams and intuition. Water's nurturing and receptive nature supports you to be adaptable, to surrender and release, expressing your emotions so there is a flow of energy and balance between your inner and outer worlds. Grief and healing rituals are Water's domain. Including a bowl of water, shells or sea-smoothed pebbles as part of your ritual, asking for the spirit of Water to help you trust your intuition and stay connected with your feelings, or washing your hands as part of the preparation process are some ways you can incorporate water into your ritual. Refer to the key qualities at the end of each seasonal chapter in Part III for a summary of associations and symbols.

Symbols, myth and archetypes

For rituals to resonate at the level of the soul, they need to communicate in the soul's language of myth, metaphor and symbolism, the stuff that dreams and stories are made of. Weaving symbols that feel alive and resonant into your ritual will engage your imagination and unconscious mind, acting as vehicles through which you can open up to other levels of reality and meaning, including the profound and primitive memory of the collective unconscious.[10] This connection with the spiritual dimension enables unseen forces to be activated that can be harnessed to energise the creative process.

A symbol is a pattern that enables you to communicate multiple levels of meaning, speaking to your unconscious mind in ways that words cannot. They act as a signifier for something else, which will be interpreted differently according to your cultural and personal background. For example, a snake has diversely been seen as a symbol of transformation and rebirth, earthly feminine power, danger and deceit, and good health. I often work with the symbol of the spiral because it points towards an archetypal path of growth, transformation and psychological or spiritual journey. Eggs and seeds are also frequently woven into my rituals to symbolise the potential and dreams within that are incubating in the darkness, preparing to be birthed through me. When you include symbols as part of your ritual, consider what meaning they carry for you so you can invoke these energies intentionally.

According to psychiatrist Carl Jung's interpretation, an archetype is an overarching pattern of behaviour that is seen recurring through myth, through which universal concepts are conveyed. Mythical figures and deities that personify these patterns of behaviour can be incorporated into your ritual to help you access the hidden aspects within you that seek liberation. A ritual provides a space for you to confront the patterning object and ask yourself 'what do I need to do to make this'? Working with the king or queen archetype in a ritual, for instance, you can invoke the qualities of sovereignty, leadership and decisiveness, to support you in making a commitment to a new path of action.

Whether you are including an image or object on your ritual altar, invoking an archetype or recreating a myth through the storytelling of your ritual, each symbol is a key to unlock deeper levels of meaning and expression. Over time, you will become familiar with the symbols that carry most resonance for you, which can be translated into your ritual signature. If a symbol, archetype or myth is calling to you or appearing repeatedly in your life, a ritual space will enable you to unravel the different layers of meaning and intentionally connect with and explore the energies moving through you and let them work on you in a safe container. Through this path of soul-making, the ritual life unveils what is buried in the shadow-self so you can access your hidden gifts and creative potential, give voice to your longing and embody your deepest truth.

Ancestors

Just as in any meaningful relationship, the bonds with our ancestors call for care and renewal. Connecting with them through ritual is a powerful way to enhance your appreciation of their influence in your life and the ways you can attend to them to bring healing to you and your family lineage.

At the beginning of your ritual, when you welcome the energies that you wish to guide your process, you can call upon your wise, kind and loving ancestors to be present in spirit and receive the blessings of your offerings. You can choose to connect with those from way back; before the time when their lineage and traditions were interrupted and they were indigenous to the land, so you can draw directly from their source of wisdom to inspire your ritual craft. Or perhaps you have a relative who died more recently, and you feel there are things left unsaid that you wish to create the space to speak about.

You may also feel drawn to those spiritual or soul ancestors who you feel a particular resonance with, who conjure specific qualities you want to express in your ritual, human and more than human. Saint Francis of Assisi, Boudicca, Jim Morrison, the Callanish Stones and Nina Simone have all been beckoned into my rituals over the years! When you consider that the bones of all your living ancestors, the decomposing wood and leaves of trees and plants, and all the dead matter of nature returns to the earth to be recycled and bring forth new life, you see your ancestors everywhere in the world around you. Feeding the dead with songs, stories, prayers, ritual feasts and delicious offerings will resource them to play a more active role in your life, bringing untold blessings, a deep sense of belonging and insights into who you truly are. Take a look at the autumn ritual 'Tending the Roots' (page 156) for an example of connecting with your ancestors in ritual space.

Carefully and consciously opening up the channel of communication with your ancestors through ritual is a vital part of remembering your wholeness, of calling back parts of yourself, healing ancestral trauma, and creating balance between the living and the dead.

Ancestral rituals can be deeply transformative, but they do require great care, humility and discernment. There are ancestors who are not healthy or wise, who can be deceptive, disruptive and even dangerous to engage with. You may prefer to seek experienced guides and elders to support you on this journey, or learn inherited rituals from wisdom-keepers that are part of your lineage, to ensure you have a safe container to open up to the ancestral realms.

The Five Branches each provide a starting point for you to consider the form, intention and flavour of the rituals you create so that your ritual life can evolve to become an authentic expression of your soul's longing. The seasonal rituals I offer later in the book will demonstrate how these branches can inform ritual design, to give you a sense of the ways they can inspire your intention. For now, let's open the way for your ritual life to begin.

Endnotes

[1] In analytical psychology, the shadow-self can include everything outside of the light of consciousness – both the unconscious, hidden aspects of the personality that the ego does not identify with, and the collective unconscious, encompassing the soul of humanity.

[2] The feminine and masculine principles are energies that are alive in each of us, interacting to create life. If they are not balanced – when one dominates at the expense of the other – disharmony and disease are the result. For life to flourish we need both: the inclusive, embodied, generative and nurturing feminine and the dynamic, potent, penetrative masculine. Through their fundamental pursuit of wholeness, rituals depend upon the qualities and patterns of behaviour that honour process, intuition, love, reciprocity, nurture, transition, healing, death, incubation, and collaboration, associated with the feminine principle, married with the focused intention and ingenuity found within the masculine principle.

[3] The more-than-human worlds encompass all beings who are not human in present physical form, including the animal, plant and Elemental realms and the invisible world of spirit – the objects and powers that exist whether or not they are experienced, including ancestors, angels, spirit guides, devas and faerie folk.

[4] The Tree of Life is a fundamental archetype in many of the world's mythologies, religious and philosophical traditions, also known as the Tree of Knowledge, Tree of Immortality, Cosmic Tree and *Yggdrasil* in Norse cosmology. The symbol reveals the structure of the Universe, pointing towards the various, interconnecting levels of existence, with the physical world we know and inhabit as just one of many dimensions occurring at the same time.

[5] Universal consciousness is connected by the vertical *Axis Mundi*, like a spine that holds together all the different parts of the body. Cross-culturally the *Axis Mundi* is expressed in different symbols, as a tree, mountain, vine, totem pole, pillar or spire, creating a bridge between the cosmic poles where the divine and mundane worlds intersect, a reflection of the macrocosm in the microcosm. It has become a universal psychological centre where chaos can be ordered within the whole and a connection made with the eternal now. In many traditions this centre is a physical place, sometimes referred to as the navel of the world – Mount Kailash in China, Uluru in Australia and the Temple Mount in Jerusalem are just a few examples.

[6] Tim 'Mac' Macartney, 'The Children's Fire', recorded live at QI Global Summit, Singapore, 2010, https://vimeo.com/20278227, (Accessed 2nd June 2020), and expanded upon in conversation with Mac (30th September 2021).

[7] There are many versions of lunar calendars that align the thirteen moons to the solar year, with each lunar cycle connected to a different tree. The system I work with is by Dusty Miller, provided courtesy of Jay and Kestrel Oakwood at The Bridget Healing Centre, Glastonbury.

[8] Jim Robbins, 'Ecopsychology: How Immersion in Nature Benefits Your Health', *Yale Environment 360*, Yale School of the Environment, January 9th 2020, https://e360.yale.edu/features/ecopsychology-how-immersion-in-nature-benefits-your-health, (Accessed 5th June 2021).

[9] In addition to the mythological Earth goddess Gaia, symbol of the Great Earth Mother, the 'Gaia' hypothesis was proposed by chemist James Lovelock in 1970, describing the Earth as a living being, self-regulating the elements to sustain life on it. I use 'Gaia' here to encompass the animated, holistic, intelligent Earth and all life that is entwined.

[10] The 'collective unconscious' was coined by Carl Jung as a way of explaining the ubiquity of psychological phenomena that could not be explained on the basis of personal experience. It refers to a structural layer of the unconscious human psyche that contains inherited elements and archetypes of the whole spiritual heritage of human's evolution.

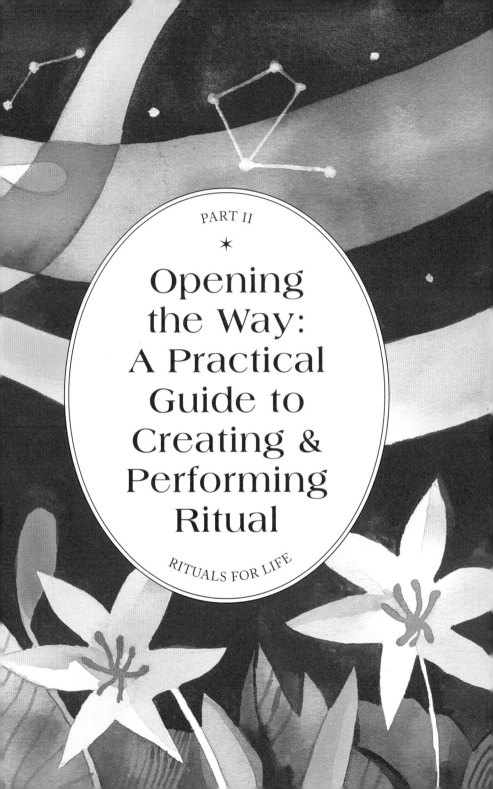

✴

PART II

Opening the Way: A Practical Guide to Creating & Performing Ritual

RITUALS FOR LIFE

Preparing the Ground

The second part of this book will support you with crafting your own rituals by exploring the fundamentals of ritual design and how to create a sacred space. This is followed by an explanation of the Four Seeds – intention, creativity, gratitude and kindness – that offer a clear framework for the ritual life and for any ritual you design. I will guide you through the practical considerations that create a strong foundation for the ritual life:

- Choosing which seasonal energy to work with
- Selecting which ritual to perform when
- How to get the most from the rituals
- Getting ready for ritual crafting: including mind, body and spirit (diet, breath, movement, sound, cleansing), plant and tree allies and ritual tools
- Creating a ritual space: including casting a circle, declaration of intention, invocation and protection, and creative design
- Closing a ritual
- Making a ritual of your own

Choosing which seasonal energy to work with

When you feel inspired to create a ritual, first consider your intention by asking these questions:

Why do you feel drawn to creating this ritual? What is happening, has happened or is about to happen that feels significant or inspires you?

What is the purpose of this ritual? What do you wish to feel and receive? What do you hope to see manifest or accomplished? How will it benefit you and others?

What inspiration, myth and symbols feel resonant for this ritual?

How relational do you want the ritual to be? Will you be alone or invite others? Who are the more-than-humans you wish to be present?

When you have refined your intention, you can usually discern whether it relates to one of the following four delineations and the corresponding season:

HONOURING BEGINNINGS AND
CREATING NEW PATHWAYS – SPRING

Including – New job, home, family member, work project, relationship status, name, commitment to self/other, wellbeing practice; visioning a new future.

Focus – Fertility, birth, intention, visioning, cleansing, renewal, expansion, dynamism, empowerment.

CELEBRATING TRANSITIONS,
GROWTH AND PARTNERSHIPS – SUMMER

Including – Weddings, vow renewals and hand-fastings; honouring new partnerships; celebrations of achievements; coming of age ceremonies and transitions such as starting school, beginning menstruation, leaving home, becoming a parent, becoming an elder.

Focus – Celebrations, union, creativity, sensuality, growth, fulfilment, expression, community.

GIVING THANKS AND
GRIEVING LOSS – AUTUMN

Including – Thanksgiving rituals for the natural world, our community and ourselves; acknowledging what we are harvesting in our lives; anniversaries; working with loss and grieving a loved one, unborn baby, relationship, unmet expectations, or body changes.

Focus – Release, letting go, cycles, grief, gratitude, acceptance, appreciation, ancestors.

HONOURING ENDINGS
AND HEALING FEARS – WINTER

Including – Healing rituals to work with fear, trauma, terminal illness, addiction, depression; initiation; honouring the death of another or a part of yourself; connecting with the Earth.

Focus – Healing, transformation, dreaming, remembering, protection, belonging, initiation, death and rebirth, reflection, wisdom.

As each season naturally blends into the next, the same goes for rituals inspired by the natural world. There is a fluidity, and sometimes a combination of two seasons will feel most fitting for your intention. Sometimes the grief and shedding of autumn will merge with the qualities of remembering and blessing the life of someone you have lost, associated with winter. Connect with your wild edges and welcome an intuitive and adaptable approach that is open to exploration and experiment.

Selecting which ritual to perform when

By attuning to the seasonal cycles, you draw upon the power of the natural world, receiving boundless support to help create the outcome you wish for. You can choose to perform your ritual during the season it most resonates with or request in your invocation that the spirit of the season and their supportive energies are present throughout your ritual. In addition to seasonal changes, the Moon and Sun cycles offer plenty of opportunities to connect with the natural forces. So too does the menstruation cycle for women, as follows:

SEASONAL RITUALS

Spring rituals – Supported by the energy of the new and waxing moon. Dawn and early morning. The follicular phase of a woman's cycle.

Summer rituals – Strengthened by the full moon. Midday and early afternoon light or in the moonlight. The ovulation phase of a woman's cycle.

Autumn rituals – Setting the intention to release at the full moon and through the waning phase. Late afternoon, early evening. Luteal or premenstrual phase of the menstrual cycle.

Winter rituals – The dark moon. Evening, night-time. Menstruation phase.

How to get the most from the rituals

Read through the ritual in Part III that you wish to create to get a feel of it. Notice if it brings up any emotions, thoughts or ideas. Use your imagination to dream into the ritual and see how it might look. Consider where you might like to perform it – is there a sanctuary in nature you love or a place in your home that feels fitting?

Choose a time to perform your ritual that is appropriate to its intent, setting aside enough time to prepare yourself and create a sacred space, also allowing time afterwards to ground and integrate your experience.

Ensure you have everything you need for the ritual before you begin. Turn off your phone and eliminate distractions so you are able to be fully present. I encourage you to find a beautiful journal to devote to your ritual journey so that you can jot down ideas and images that come to mind before you craft your ritual space, and for recording your experience once the journey is complete.

Getting Ready for Ritual Crafting

Mind, body and spirit

In order to become receptive to the subtleties of energy weaving through your ritual and your intuitive wisdom, there are helpful ways to prepare your body as a vessel. These preparations also cultivate awareness about how you relate to yourself and approach your ritual life. Creating an effective ritual to prepare yourself for entering sacred space, that you repeat often, will create clear pathways that make it easier and quicker to shift your consciousness and help you feel centred and aligned to a higher sense of self.

You can change your consciousness in simple and effective ways to ensure you are not preoccupied with your thoughts or detached from your body.

Diet

Becoming aware of the food you eat, how it nourishes you and feels in your body, is a vital act of self-care, integral to living a ritual life. Your relationship with food and your body is key to understanding your relationship with the Earth, the physical world. Recognising your body as a complex ecosystem that responds to how you care for it brings an attentiveness that translates to your ritual life.

Imagine you are a vessel; you wish to arrive empty at the ritual doorway so there is space within to be filled with inspiration. This applies to your body and mind. Choosing carefully to consume only vital, alive foods on the day of your ritual and avoiding dulling carbohydrates, heavy fats or rich meats will ensure your body is ripe for energy work. It is traditional in many cultures to fast as part of ritual preparation or for the duration of the ritual, for up to four days in the case of the Native American Vision Quest. Fasting is a powerful way to connect with a sense of lightness and emptiness, enhance your sensitivity, quieten the mind and help dissolve the sense of separation between your body and the world around you.

Breath

Breath techniques have been used for thousands of years to bring about altered states of consciousness. Slowing your breath and deepening it into your belly will encourage a softening and a sense of calm that centres you in your body. Breathing intentionally into your heart and feeling your heart space expand connects you to the qualities of love and compassion. Speeding up your breathing using the 'breath of fire', or other activating techniques, will fill you with vital energy and heighten awareness.

I often begin a ritual by taking three deeper, conscious breaths to become present with my experience and embodied in the space. Try different breaths to see what helps you feel centred and works with your intention and the type of ritual you wish to create.

Movement

One of the more playful ways to prepare for entering sacred space is to dance, preferably to music with plenty of rhythm. Dancing helps get you out of your thinking head and into your sensual body, releases tension and increases blood flow, bringing a vitality to your ritual presence. It also stirs the release of the 'happy hormones' serotonin and dopamine, lifting and lightening your mood. You can bring more intense emotions into your sacred space if they need to be tended to, such as in a grief ritual or memorial for a loved one. In this case you might prefer to dance with these emotions, using your body to express the stirrings in your heart.

A lively body shake-out, exuberant skip, or more gentle practices such as qigong and yoga can also be enjoyed as part of your ritual warm-up.

Sound

Working on a vibrational level, sound is a dynamic way to help shift energy and consciousness. Drumming is one of the most fundamental tools for medicine folk, enabling them to dance between realms using the rhythm. You can drum for yourself or use a recorded track of a repetitive drum beat to help change your state of consciousness. A rattle can also be used for this purpose, and other rhythmic instruments, such as a gong, kalimba, guitar and shruti box, can create more meditative and focused attention. You might know some specific songs that really switch you on. Play around and notice what effect different sounds have on your perception and sense of embodied presence.

Our own voices can be just as potent for inducing altered states, and are something we can all use, no matter where we are. When we sing, healing vibrations move through us and our oxygen intake is increased, activating our cells and clearing the mind. Using mantras or singing rhythmically for a period of time can quickly change your mood and energetic frequency.

Cleansing

Purifying your body, ceremonial tools and the physical space by cleansing with the elements before beginning a ritual is a powerful way to enhance your sense of entering sacred space and ensuring the energy is clear. Refer to the spring ritual 'Cleansing with the Elements', page 76, for an extended cleansing process.

You can use herbs and resins for cleansing, also known as 'smudging', by lighting a bundle of dried herbs or placing some on a piece of charcoal as you offer your gratitude to the spirit of the plant or tree. Then use your hands or a feather to waft the scented smoke around your body, under your arms and feet and between your legs. If you are using any ritual tools, such as a drum or rattle, and any other physical elements you are using in your ritual, you can extend the smudging around them too. Whether indoors or in an open space, clearing the environment by circulating this sacred smoke – being sure to get into the corners and nooks and crannies – will strengthen your ritual container and energetic protection.

Another way I enjoy cleansing with the help of our plant allies is to tie together a bundle of birch twigs, rosemary, willow or mugwort and use it like a brush, sweeping and gently tapping the bundle up and down my body or around the boundary of my ritual space. As each plant is activated they release a delicious scent, infusing the air around you.

Water is a powerful transmitter of energy, and by sprinkling spring water around your body, tools and space you can achieve the same effect as with smudging.

Sound works on a vibrational level so using your voice with focused intention, beating your drum, using a gong or shaking your rattle around your ritual space are all effective ways of clearing the energy. When I feel called to craft an impromptu ritual, I sometimes just clap my hands three times, visualising the energy around me activating and clarifying.

Plant and tree allies for cleansing and offerings

Working with plant and tree spirits as part of your cleansing practices, gathering them as medicine or to create a store of offerings for your rituals and journeys, invites you to become more intimate with them and learn their language. Nurturing your relationship with native plants honours the spirit of the land you live with and strengthens the resonance of its medicine, so always aim to work with ethically sourced, sustainable, native plants. Over time you will notice which plants you are drawn to work with, whose smell evokes something in you, that you can use in your rituals more frequently.

If you are able to, harvesting your own sacred herbs will greatly enhance your appreciation of their qualities. You can make a ritual of your gathering, asking the spirits of the plant or tree to guide you to them, harvesting them where they grow in abundance, and leaving an offering or sharing a song and prayer to thank them for their generosity and medicine. You can also cultivate these plants yourself, growing them in pots on your windowsill or designating an area of your garden to your sacred plants, imbuing them with your love and care as you watch them grow.

Dry the plants at home by hanging them in bundles, and then crumble or cut them into smaller pieces before storing them in jars. You can also create your own smudge sticks by holding a bundle of fresh, aromatic plants together, wrap around the stalks with natural cotton string, then crisscross the string over and under the bundle and tie to secure. You can use them once dry.

Below are some of the plant allies I work with. I make smudge sticks combining cedar and rosemary that I find very effective for purifying a space prior to a ritual, but you can explore what works for you.

Cedar (*Cedrus* family) helps to cultivate spiritual strength and stamina; a wonderful herb to work with for longer rituals and sacred quests. Provides cleansing and protection.

Lavender (*Lavandula* family) creates a harmonious and peaceful atmosphere, attracting loving energy and encouraging a restful mind. Promotes clear vision, purpose and intention.

Meadowsweet (*Filipendula ulmaria*) enhances a sense of calm and openness, stimulates intuition and connects you with the qualities of love and joy by softening a hardened heart.

Mugwort (*Artemisia vulgaris*) has a long history of being used for ritual preparation as a powerful herb to aid lucid dreaming and communication with the ancestral realms. An empowering and strengthening herb, helpful with balancing more intense emotions.

Rose (*Rosa* family) is a powerful tonic for your heart chakra, helping to open you up to both giving and receiving unconditional love. Supports your full expression and inner radiance to shine.

Rosemary (*Salvia rosmarinus*) is an aromatic purifying herb, beneficial for mental clarity, enhancing memory and protection.

Sage (*Salvia officinalis*) is a potent herb for purification and cleansing, removing unwanted energies and improving concentration. Choose a native variety.

Thyme (*Thymus vulgaris*) helps with dissipating negative emotions, raising your energy levels and spiritual stamina.

Yarrow (*Achillea millefolium*) encourages peace, serenity and a connection with our inner wisdom. A powerful protective herb that wards off negative energy.

Ritual tools

All you ultimately need for any ritual is your body, breath, clarity of intention and the willingness to connect with your heart. As one of my mentors once told me, 'Everything you need is within you. The rest is just superfluous.' If, however, like me, you enjoy creating beauty, feeling the textures of stone, clay and bone, and come alive with the scent of meadowsweet or pine, you will most likely be drawn towards adding items to your ritual toolbox.

Ritual objects can be anything that inspires you, is charged with sacred meaning, carrying a story or sentiment. On one level these items are made ritual items by your intention for them to be so, but they also become imbued with your essence the more you use them.

You may want to invest in a lantern for using candles outdoors, a ceremonial shawl or a beautiful ceramic bowl. I recommend investing in handmade items to maintain a thread of connection with the maker and the raw materials. Handmade objects carry more life and intention than mass-produced ones, and there is a more direct relationship with the creative process that will encourage your own creative juices to flow.

Creating a Ritual Space

With experience you will discover ways that feel natural for you to begin your rituals. You create sacred space around you by creating it *within* you, so the key is to cultivate ways that instil an open-hearted and reverential presence you can access readily. Whether it is lighting a candle, singing, placing a shawl on your shoulders or feeling your feet rooted in the earth, you can create sacred space quickly with clear intention.

Casting a circle to begin a ritual has been a practice of medicine folk from native traditions around the world for generations, as a universal symbol that creates harmony and union. The circle is the perfect container to hold energy in motion. With no beginning or end, it creates a portal, a space out of time that is open to the cosmic forces all spinning their own circular dance.

The circle is cast to allow the energy to flow and transform in a safe way, ensuring that anything that happens within that space remains there once the circle is closed. By defining and consecrating the ritual space, there is a sense of enclosure and a change in energy between inside/outside. You can create a circle around you, either energetically in your mind's eye or drawing or marking one with scarves, chairs, flowers, or foliage. To imbue the circle with power and creative energy, you welcome the directions, Elements and all those you wish to be present. If you are facilitating a community gathering this process can be done before others arrive or invite the participants to join you as part of the ritual. It is vital to begin with a short grounding exercise or visualisation, ensuring all present have arrived fully and feel united together.

I offer here an extended example of how to open sacred space, but it could simply involve acknowledging the directions by bowing to them or drawing an imaginary circle around your ritual area.

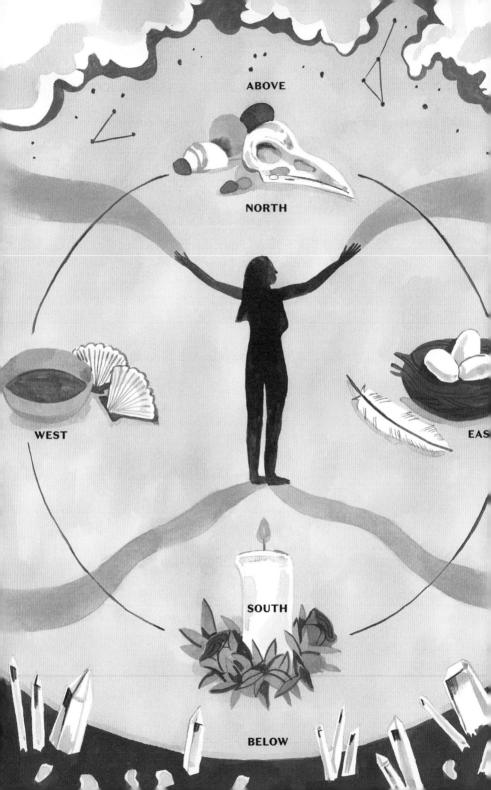

Casting a circle

Begin by closing your eyes and focusing on your body. Expand your breath into your heart and then down to your belly as you let out a sigh as you exhale.

Feel your feet rooted down through the earth. Imagine your crown chakra at the top of your head opening to the Cosmos and the golden light of the Sun pouring downwards, infusing your heart.

Rub your hands together to activate your palms and hold in a prayer position as you speak from your heart:

'From this place between earth and sky, with the greatest love, honour and gratitude, I open sacred space. I give thanks to the spirit of place for holding me here and ask your permission to carry out this ritual.'

Listen inwardly for a response or pay attention to any signs from the natural world that indicate a 'yes' or 'no'. Respect the answer!

If the answer is 'yes', turn to the east, direction of the rising sun, raise your arms up and speak:

'Spirit of the east, Element of Air, realm of my winged kin, I welcome you here. Thank you for this sacred breath. May you infuse my words with love as I speak from my heart and listen with curiosity and attentiveness to the wisdom within all things. May you bring clarity to my thoughts so that I am fully present here, focused on my intention, open to receive inspiration and communicate my truth.'

Bow to the east.

Turn to the south, direction of the midday sun, raise your arms up and speak:

'Spirit of the south, Element of Fire, I welcome you here. Thank you for your vibrant, transformative energy and purifying power. May you clear away all obstacles so that I show up fully, express myself faithfully, and come into right relationship with my power. Help me to tend to my inner flame, playfully explore my creativity and align with my purpose through this ritual.'

Bow to the south.

Turn to the west, direction of the setting sun, raise your arms and speak:

'Spirit of the west, Element of Water, realm of my finned kin, I welcome you here. Thank you for showing me how to surrender

and flow with the Great River of Life. May you guide me through
this ritual, helping me to honour my intuition and dance with the
unknown. Show me how to adapt and express my gratitude in ways
that are fully felt and received by others.'
Bow to the west.

Turn to the north, the realm of night-time and darkness, raise your
arms up and speak:
> *'Spirit of the north, Element of Earth, the realm of my wise and*
> *benevolent ancestors and animal kin, I welcome you here. Thank you*
> *for your deep and tender holding, for your generosity and abundance.*
> *May you support my full embodiment and integration of this ritual,*
> *enabling me to overcome fear and experience the depth of my belonging*
> *to this beautiful Earth. Show me how to be kind and accepting of all*
> *that arises, patient and willing to see things differently.'*

Bow to the north.

Look up to the skies, raise your arms up and speak:
> *'Welcoming all that is above, the star beings, angels, ascended masters,*
> *all the guides that love me. Thank you for shining the light of truth*
> *and blessing me with inspiration. May you guide me through this*
> *ritual and help me open up to be a vessel for love, in service to life.'*

Bow to all that is above.

Kneeling on the earth with your hands touching the soil, speak aloud:
> *'Welcoming all that is below, the spirits of the plant beings, roots*
> *and mycelium, minerals and crystals, the elementals and devas, and*
> *the spirit of the land here. Thank you for your strength and wisdom.*
> *May you help renew my commitment and willingness to explore the*
> *darkness and connect me with the natural intelligence within all life.'*

Bow your head to the earth.

Standing with one hand on your heart, the other on your belly,
speak aloud:
> *'Welcoming all that is at the centre, the love in my heart, the wisdom*
> *in my DNA, the memory in my blood and bones, the light and the*

dark, the full spectrum of my being. May I be in harmony with all life,
celebrating the mystery of creation and the potential within all things
as I offer myself in service for the greatest good.'
Bow your head towards your heart and say, *'Blessed be.'*

Your circle is now cast!

Declaration of intention, invocation and protection

With the ritual space opened you now need to infuse the container
with the energy of your intention by stating it clearly and concisely
(see 'the Four Seeds', page 58, for a detailed description of setting your
intention). As part of your intention, include the wish for your ritual to
be dedicated to the highest good to ensure a harmonious outcome that
is of benefit to all beings everywhere. Acknowledge and give thanks to
the spirit of the place where you are carrying out the ritual, including
the ancestors, guardians, plant spirits and animal kin who are present.
As you state your intention, now is the moment to light a candle or
hold a bowl of water as you speak to infuse the water with your words.

With the ritual container in place, you can summon energies that are
greater than yourself, the invisible powers, archetypes, ancestors and guides
that you wish to be present for this rite. You may have familiar helpers and
angels you work with regularly and there may be those that you invite for
their unique gifts and energy that are relevant to your ritual. Be experimen-
tal with how you go about your invocation, as who you invoke informs how
you invoke them so it might take time to find ways that resonate; what gets
their attention and whether they like specific offerings.

The key is to be authentic and heartfelt, even vulnerable, as you share
your longing and sincerity. Invite the energies to join you as though you
are speaking to an elder or friend, creating a connection that is loving
and honourable. Speak with respect, asking whoever you have called
upon to create a layer of protection around your space, asserting clear
boundaries that any uninvited energies that are harmful or destructive
are not welcome.

Conclude your invocation when you notice subtle shifts in the
energetic field or feel a sense of connection with these powers.

Creative design

Once the stage is set, your ritual can take any form. Just ensure your ears and heart are open; listening to receive inspiration from the powers you have invoked and to hear your own inner wisdom speak. Allow space for silence. Move in the direction of your intention as you attend to the energetic forces at play, responding with curiosity and the willingness to trust in what naturally arises. Be guided by the sensations and feelings in your body as this is the language that you have the capacity to interpret for yourself. Refer to the seed of creativity, page 61, for more insight into this part of the ritual, and use the seasonal rituals as a reference, going on to explore ways to make them your own, adding your unique flavour and symbols that resonate for you.

Closing a ritual

When you feel that your ritual has come to a natural conclusion it is important to close the space to create a container around the energetic work and ensure you ground fully in your body before carrying on with your day.

There are various ways you can do this, beginning with acknowledging and thanking the powers and guides that were present in a heartfelt way, releasing them, and offering up the blessings created from your ritual to the wider Web of Life in a gesture of kindness and appreciation. You might make symbolic offerings, such as leaving food or water for the spirit of the place that held you through your ritual, or ask that the love and good feelings be carried out to touch the hearts of others. Close the space by going anti-clockwise around, thanking the Elements and directions for their support and transformational energies.

You can then use one of the Elements to help clear the ritual space, as you did for the cleansing preparation. Blowing out your candle is one of the quickest ways to conclude your work, or if you are in a group you might like to sing a song collectively as you hold hands and then break them.

Grounding and integration

When your ritual is complete, you need to intentionally ground yourself so that your energy sphere is closed down and you are ready to embrace the rest of your day in an embodied way. Practising good energy hygiene is a vital part of the ritual life.

I like to give my body a good shake, clap or jump up and down a few times, feel my feet on the ground and look around me at my immediate environment to inhabit the physical space again. I check in with how I am feeling and smudge herbs, wash my hands or sprinkle water on my face to cleanse my energetic field if necessary.

It can be helpful to have some earthing food – root vegetables or a hearty, warm broth. This can be a wonderful way to continue the celebration if you are with a group of people. Always be sure to drink plenty of water throughout the rest of the day, as with any healing work. Enjoy a cleansing salt bath or some barefoot walking to further help you land if need be.

You might choose to journal about your experiences or use a voice recorder to share any feelings, inspiration or insights. Was there anything you committed to that you can write down and reaffirm by speaking aloud for the duration of the next lunar cycle? Revisit these journal entries over time to help embed the experience and integrate the healing or insight that occurred.

Making a ritual of your own

To begin with you might choose to follow the rituals in this book, although there is ample space for your own creativity and intuition to guide you in a different direction and there is always the potential for unexpected happenings when you are weaving with the spirit realms.

With experience you will find ways of crafting that feel more instinctual for you, and I whole-heartedly encourage you to listen to your natural urges and ideas for they will lead to understanding your ritual signature and personal power. True alchemy comes when you collaborate with the spirit world by paying attention to the subtle energies of the ritual space you have created. As you grow in confidence, allow yourself to be infused with the inspiration that comes in any given moment to create a ritual that is responsive to the moment you are in and the environment that surrounds you.

Spontaneous rituals can feel exciting, perhaps a little edgy, and require a leap of faith to embrace the unknown. Some of my most memorable rituals began by opening up to a landscape or sacred site, or from the triggering of an intense emotion that compelled me to listen and make space for honouring, remembering, celebrating or releasing.

Keys to the Ritual Life:
The Four Seeds

Through my exploration of ritual, I have found that the Elements provide keys to open up another dimension of ritual design that I have come to call the Four Seeds. When you plant these seeds in your rituals it will help them to flourish and take root in your life, cultivating pathways towards a more meaningful existence. Their innate qualities help to create a simple and balanced framework you can adopt for any ritual, while giving you the freedom to follow your intuition and dance with the creative energies present. You can also work more broadly on nurturing these four qualities in your everyday life, so you develop the confidence to explore them more deeply in your rituals.

THE FOUR SEEDS OF RITUAL
• INTENTION
• CREATIVITY
• GRATITUDE
• KINDNESS

KINDNESS

INTENTION

GRATITUDE

CREATIVITY

All the seasonal rituals in Part III include the Four Seeds as they have become the formula I use in any ritual design. It is helpful to explore them here so that you have a sense of how they can inform a ritual process and relate to the four Elements.

Starting with the activating Element of **Air in the east**, you use your voice to state your **intention**, the guiding force of the ritual.

With your direction clear, space opens for your **creativity** to flourish as you dance with the **Fires of the south** and collaborate with the invisible forces to forge something beautiful in response to your intention.

In response to such beauty, you are moved by **Water in the west** to share your **gratitude** for what fed and inspired you through your ritual, and all those you are supported by in your life.

With your heart full, you come to rest with the **Earth in the north** and share your blessings of **kindness** and make offerings that ripple outwards to the wider Earth community so others may benefit from your ritual.

The harvest from your ritual contains within it the seeds to take forward in your life that have grown from your intention, so you can decide on the next step that will continue to support its manifestation, returning to the east to mark a new beginning.

To demonstrate how the Four Seeds can be included in your rituals, I expand on them here and offer playful invitations to help you refine your understanding of how they can flourish as part of your ritual life. You can explore the invitations at any time to enrich your sense of their energy and enhance their presence in your life. They can also be done before a ritual to help you gain more clarity on it or be incorporated into your ritual.

I. The power of intention

The primary ingredient for creating effective ritual is the guiding force of intention. What are you hoping to do and achieve with your ritual? What do you imagine to be a positive outcome?

In the domain of Air, intention is connected with the invisible realms of mind, inspiration, intuition and imagination, which combine to create an image or idea that acts like a blueprint for what you want to embody. Holding this image in your mind and compressing your intention into words enfold creative power, guiding the energy to flow into physical form. With a clear intention, you are directing your arrow with wilful direction and drawing upon the power of the bow to ensure the best outcome for your ritual. A declaration made in ritual space not only helps heal you – it ripples out through your life and your lineage, into the past and future.

Your power comes from the alignment of mind (will), heart (body) and voice (soul) as you stand in your truth. To bring your full power to your intention it is necessary to ask what is the deeper motivation behind it that flows through your life? Do you want to embody your full potential in order to be of most use to others, for example? When you bring your intention to what is truly needed and what gifts you have to offer, you will access the wellspring of potential that comes from the river of your longing.

With any ritual you craft, it is vital to state your intention to begin the process of gathering in the supportive energies you need to help you fulfil what you wish for. To engage their attention, you need to use your voice to create vibrations that will ripple outwards into the Web of Life. Words are the vibrations of nature and the keys to activate change. Grounding yourself through your body, quietening your mind and drawing in some deeper breaths, ensures you are fully present so that your words come forth in a precise way.

INVITATIONS TO REFINE INTENTION

Medicine walk – Go for a walk as you hold the question 'what is my intention for this ritual?' and pay attention to any intuitive responses that come forth as well as any signs from the world around you.

Journalling – To distil down your intention it can be helpful to journal and ask questions about your motivation and hopes for the ritual beforehand.

Listening practice – Holding a stone or other natural object, what do you hear in response to a question or request for guidance about your ritual?

Write a letter from your older self to your present self – Imagine you are further along your life path, embodying wisdom and purpose. What does this future version of you have to say to you now that might shed light on your motivation and deeper longing?

Finding your voice – Record yourself free-associating around questions, dreams and ideas, or practise speaking an invocation for a ritual to become more comfortable with your voice and use of words.

II. The joy of creativity

Creativity is the fundamental quality inherent in nature that is responsible for all life coming into being, and what this beautiful world tells me about the nature of existence is that it is created with love. To create with love, you need to welcome your inner child and artist into ritual space and feed them with beauty, inspiration and devotion; giving them the resources and freedom to create will provide a space for play, spontaneity and curiosity. When you remove the obstacles to your creativity, the Element of Fire can burn brightly and provide the dynamic energy needed to activate your ideas into form.

Engaging your sensory body, coming into a state of childlike innocence and following your joy and desires will help you go beyond self-limiting beliefs about your creative abilities and engage in this beautiful dance with the invisible, so that you can share your soul with the world. The art of ritual comes from the communication between the individual soul, the collective soul of the Earth, and the sacred or transpersonal soul, creating a dynamic conversation that becomes the heart of your ritual and infuses your life with beauty. This is the joyful part of a ritual that might look like sculpting a clay vessel, creating a mandala of flowers, painting a mask, dressing up and dancing, weaving an altar or story, but it also includes every sound, gesture and action that is expressed in ritual space.

As an artist you must be connected with your desires and listen to your longing, for this is where the energy of Eros will infuse your life and encourage you to take risks. Eros is the creative Earth energy that longs to express itself through you, pulling you into a conscious relationship with life. In ritual space your creativity comes from your willingness to collaborate with those energies that you have summoned and those alive in you that seek expression.

INVITATIONS TO ENRICH CREATIVITY

Singing with nature – Make spontaneous sounds in response to the landscape you are in, and sing songs to trees, rivers and birds. Practise listening to a natural object and see if you can hear their song and sing it back to them.

Feeding the flame – Take your inner artist for a date, feeding them with beauty and inspiration, and engaging your senses with pleasure.

Dancing for freedom – Use your body to communicate your feelings and emotions by moving to music and imagining your body as a paintbrush, expressing your inner world.

Flower arranging – Celebrate beauty and collaboration with nature by gathering blooms and creating floral displays to adorn your home.

Creating an altar – Explore what is alive in you, the symbols and images you resonate with, by weaving an altar with items that sing to your soul.

III. The value of gratitude

Through the process of creativity, you are turned on to the mystery and playfulness that flows through life and the many ways you are supported in birthing your dreams into reality. What naturally arises in response to being turned on and feeling a part of this miraculous gift of life is gratitude, and a deep trust in the process of living, creating and loving.

When you realise the extent that you are appreciated and upheld by the greater Web of Life you can surrender your attachments, let go of limiting fears and give generously of yourself, knowing you are cared for on the deepest level. Feeling grateful is an internal experience of fullness and expansion in the heart that arises from this recognition of love and connection, inspired by the Element of Water. Devotion and prayer flow from this state of being as you tune into your emotions and express them as a gesture of gratitude, dissolving the boundaries between yourself and the world. Grief is another aspect of gratitude – as you mourn for the loss of what you love you are also giving thanks for what was.

By expressing your gratitude or grief through words, actions and songs as part of a ritual, you are acknowledging and giving something back to the energies, beings and resources that are helping bring about a positive outcome for your ritual, feeding them with your praise and prayers. Like the ripples across the surface of water, your gratitude circulates outwards, touching the hearts of others. The ritual life will help you appreciate the value of sharing your gratitude and the reciprocity inherent within nature that ensures there is a balance of giving and receiving so that all life thrives and regenerates.

INVITATIONS TO GIVE THANKS

Gratitude stone – Carry a stone in your bag or pocket and every time you see or feel it, hold it and say three things you are thankful for.

Bedtime lullaby – Soothe yourself to sleep by recalling the moments and beings that made you smile today. Hum or sing your gratitude.

Sharing gratitude with family/friends – Arrange a meal where you all give thanks for something, or send a message to someone and tell them what you are grateful for about them.

Give away – Have a clear-out of your home, donating items to charity and putting aside things for friends that you think they would love.

Water talk – Infuse a bottle of water with your loving gratitude by speaking to them about all the things you care for, that inspire you, that you want to protect. Offer the water to a river (or the earth) to ripple out into the waters of the world.

IV. The blessing of kindness

A ritual life helps to expand your perception to include the many intricate relationships that you are a part of. The illusion of separation is replaced with the recognition of belonging; you are actively participating in the creation of the future and the world needs you. This remembering may take time, but you can begin with the conscious intent to notice and foster kindness, by attending to the needs of others – whether they are a river, ancestor, faraway friend or stranger.

When you close ritual space with a form of blessing that offers love, care and protection to others, you are cultivating kindness in acknowledgement of the Web of Life that is supporting you, and that you have a mutual responsibility towards. It is the gift of the Earth Element to remind us that we reap what we sow. With the creative energy you have generated from enacting your ritual you can pay it forward by making offerings and speaking blessings, directing the energy outwards with words, gifts or actions, committing to a pledge or sending love and healing to others.

Kindness has gracious eyes, giving freely without wanting in return, unconcerned with status or competition. I believe it is the fundamental agent of change, giving meaning and value to life, fostering compassion, empathy and forgiveness in ways that can transform your relationships and experience of the world. There is a deep sweetness in offering kindness as a closing to your ritual, leaving this imprint on your heart that in some small way you have fed and enriched the lives of others and seeded something beautiful in the world.

INVITATIONS TO SHARE KINDNESS

Little notes of loveliness – Write uplifting, kind and loving messages and leave them in public places for strangers to find.

Forgive and let go – Hold a heavy stone and feel the weight of all that you have not been able to forgive in your life. Speak to the stone and share what burdens you. Throw the stone in to a river or ocean as you offer your forgiveness, freeing yourself from these burdens.

Compliment a stranger – Share something lovely about how someone made you feel or what they inspired in you.

Make a blessing pot – Write kind, loving messages and put them in a pot or bowl, to radiate outwards into your home or workplace.

Gathering offerings – Collect items in jars and pouches that can be used for offerings in your rituals, such as dried petals and herbs, oats or seeds.

Before you begin your ritual journey through the seasons, here is a reminder of how to incorporate the Four Seeds into your rituals, which you can look out for in the extended rituals in Part III:

INCORPORATING THE FOUR SEEDS

- Clarify and state your **intention** at the start of the ritual.
- Expand your awareness, open your heart, and give space for your natural **creativity** to emerge in response to your intention.
- Conclude by expressing your **gratitude** for all the beings and energies that have supported you, including the spirit of the place within which you have carried out your ritual.
- Close your ritual with blessings, offerings and acts of **kindness**, to create ripples of goodwill out into the world and Web of Life.

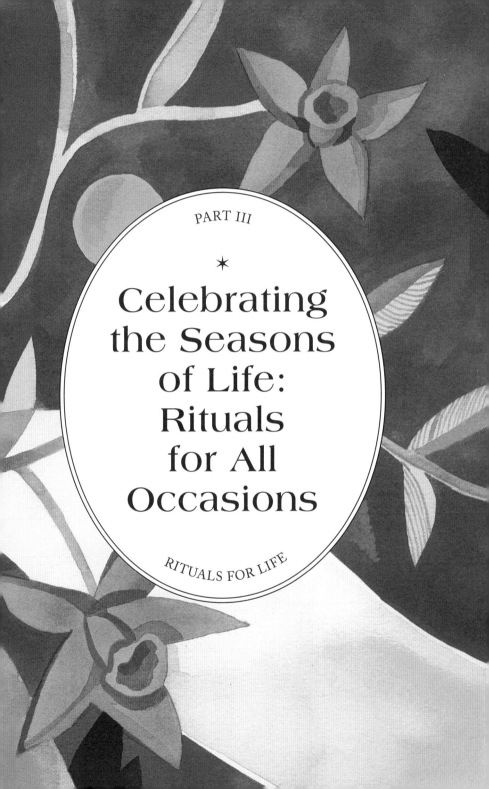

PART III

*

Celebrating
the Seasons
of Life:
Rituals
for All
Occasions

RITUALS FOR LIFE

Spring

It is through the portals of the seasons and nature's cycles that I began to appreciate the subtler forces at play within ritual design. This part of the book is based around the four seasons of spring, summer, autumn and winter because I feel they offer vital cues to understanding the natural energies that you can draw upon when you have clarified the intention for your ritual, or to inspire you to create one.

The natural world offers us a powerful reflection of our life cycles, inspiring a deeper understanding and acceptance of the transitions we go through. For example, witnessing the emergence of spring after a long winter reflects the joy and anticipation that accompany a ritual heralding a new beginning or birth, and the creative and expansive energy of summer encourages me to celebrate the fullness and achievements in my life. Watching a great old oak tree letting go of its leaves so effortlessly in the autumn wind reminds me of how to gracefully release the past and what I have outgrown. In the quiet of winter, I come home to myself and the Earth as I embrace the stillness, as does the oak, and integrate the lessons of the past cycle of growth. With an open and curious heart, you can learn to celebrate these changes and honour the fullness of your life journey in creative ways that support integration and healing.

The Dance of Spring

When I step outside in spring, I feel a renewal of hope and possibility. Bubbling within the plants, bulbs and trees is all the energy that has been stored up over winter, gathering, preparing for rebirth. The buds on the chestnut and birch trees that surround my home are bursting at the seams as the first green shoots appear through the soil, giving way to crocuses and tulips and the joyful trumpeting daffodils that seem to be bellowing their delight. The birds begin busily foraging for materials to build their nests, flitting from the drainpipes above my window to the nearby branches and hedges.

There is still a coolness in the air, sweetened by the dew and occasional frost that sprinkles the grass, ushering in a time of fertility and abundance. Walking in a beech wood after the first leaves have unfurled, I am bathed in the freshest green, so vital I feel my heart soar with gratitude for the regeneration of life around and within me.

Underfoot, once the snowdrops have withered, grow swathes of bright-green ramsons that cover whole woodlands with the softest of carpets. I love to meander through forests gathering baskets of these wild garlic leaves to make into pesto and add to soups, with all the life force stored in the earth over winter infused in their leaves providing the perfect remedy to shift stagnation and awaken me to the surging, vibrant energy of spring. A pale primrose flower plucked from the edge of the forest path, sucked on my tongue, offers a soft peachy flavour, perfect for dessert!

I often need a boost after winter to help get things moving again and rejuvenate my body. Nettles, chickweed, cleavers, dandelion and burdock all grow at the onset of spring, offering the nutritional and digestive support I need to cleanse my cells and blood, eliminate sluggishness and fill my body with wild, green medicine. I like to walk a circle around my garden as the morning rises and see what edible plants call to me, gathering some of their leaves to add to a breakfast smoothie or green juice. This morning ritual encourages me to start my day in relationship with the natural world, grounded in gratitude for the healing and inspiration this brings.

The essence of spring

Spring's awakening is like a dawn symphony of birdsong after a long, dark night; bringing a sweetness and joy to soothe my stiff body and weary mind after the harshness of winter. As woodland animals rouse from their torpor and hedgehogs, bats and dormice arise from their hibernation, us humans are also emerging from our winter cave. As the natural world is reborn, so are you. You are beginning a new dance of the spiral, preparing for a cycle of outward growth and expansion, gathering your strength from the deep roots you grew over winter and inspiration from your dreaming to curate a new chapter of your life.

The essence of this season is renewal. When the Sun rises in the east a new day begins, much like the dawning of spring signals a fresh start. As the Sun grows stronger the light and warmth infuse your cells and encourage a new phase of creativity and production. You are gifted the opportunity to begin again and create another garden, filled with your hopes for the year ahead. The phase of the lunar cycle connected with spring is the new moon, when she first appears in the darkness of the night sky, beckoning us to give birth to our dreams each month.

Spring heralds the beginning of new life and the sowing of the first seeds in gardens and fields. The seed is a powerful symbol for spring, carrying within it all the potential for life and fulfilment, waiting for the right conditions to grow and bear fruit. Much like the egg, a familiar image at this time or year associated with Easter, these seeds require care and nurturing. The fertile soil or a nest woven with love provides the crucible for your spring seeds to grow and thrive.

Spring brings with her a joyful innocence that compels you to shed your winter cloak and celebrate the pure delight of being alive. You can connect with the archetype of the child and the qualities of playfulness and curiosity to expand your imagination and potential of what's possible in your life. With childlike eyes you look upon the world with wonder and awe and a sense of adventure, looking to engage in more spontaneous and expansive ways.

Ways to attune to the energy of spring

Besides the nibbling of green leaves and sowing of seeds, you can usher in a time of renewal in your life by intentionally changing aspects of your environment and self to align with the transformative and potent energy of nature during springtime: as within, so without.

There is still time to clear away any metaphorical brambles or weeds that might impede the flourishing of your dream-seeds, creating more space for them to grow. This might involve a thorough spring clean of your home, clearing out cupboards and drawers, recycling all that is no longer of use to you, rearranging furniture or painting walls to create a fresh look. Welcome nature indoors with bunches of wildflowers and twigs of silky willow blossom. Anything that uplifts you, emboldens you, stirs you awake and connects you with appreciation, wonder and gratitude will ensure you are supporting your whole ecosystem in the most effective way.

Create a space to nurture your dreams and connect with the energy of spring – transform a windowsill or tabletop into an altar, adorned with natural items, precious objects and reminders of what you wish to grow in your life. Spring is the perfect time to energetically cleanse your home (see page 76) and to make a revitalising spray with uplifting essential oils such as lemon, orange, lemongrass and grapefruit, mixed with filtered water. I love to spritz this about my workspace before starting a new project, in my car if I am embarking on a long journey, and around any room that needs a quick clearing of energy.

In addition to your home environment, you might want to change your physical appearance with a haircut, or reimagine your style by wearing some bold, eccentric clothes that you were saving for a summer festival! Finding ways to push your comfort zone will expand your capacity for welcoming new experiences, so taking playful steps to explore different ways of expressing yourself can be immensely rewarding.

The initiatory energy of spring makes it a supportive time to begin new routines and create wellbeing practices to complement the vision you have for your best self; consider joining a new fitness class, committing to a daily meditation practice or finding a club to connect with others who share a similar passion or hobby. Follow your joy and seek out what brings you real soul-level nourishment, while listening to the needs of your body. Take an honest inventory of yourself and see what needs to change in your life so you are able to thrive.

You can create the conditions for inner wellbeing by enjoying a spring cleanse or detox, following a green diet filled with wild plants and plenty of water to flush out the toxins for a week, or omitting certain things from your diet, such as sugar, alcohol or dairy. Fasting also offers a powerful way to reset the system and can be done intermittently each day, only eating for the six hours between noon and 6pm, or by carrying out an extended fast.

The barriers to change are nearly always found in your mind and the well-trodden pathways you have created by living habitually and often unconsciously. Witnessing your thoughts without attaching to them, like clouds moving across the sky, and learning tools that help rewire your neural pathways such as meditation, can be essential allies on the path to living a ritual life.

Daily spring rituals
Greeting the dawn
Start your day in reverence and gratitude by connecting with the power of the rising Sun, giving thanks for his light blessing another day and bestowing life-giving energy to the Earth. Turn to face the east and raise your arms to make a Y-shape. Imagine rays of light pouring into the space between your arms, down your head and bathing your whole body. Ask that his light guide you through your day and that all your actions may be infused with his brilliance before bowing in gratitude.

Morning seeds
Setting an intention for your day helps steer your inner navigation system in the direction you want it to go. Begin by expressing your gratitude, before visualising your day unfolding as you would wish. Think of one word that encompasses what you want to feel today. Feel this quality in your heart and body and speak aloud 'I choose … (e.g. joy)', three times, imagining these sound vibrations rippling outwards, charging the energy field around you. Take moments throughout your day to tune back into this feeling and intention, repeating the word.

Singing your joy
Wherever you are, turn up the volume on your voice and sing something that makes you smile! You can sing along to a song you know and love or make one up, and move your body too, without any concern about how you look or sound. Sing loud and proud, enjoying opening up your chest and throat as the vibrations help you expand.

Meditation
There are many ways you can approach meditation. I like to keep it simple, sometimes poised in front of my altar or sitting with my back against a tree. Take a few deep breaths into your belly and relax a little more on each exhalation, inwardly setting your intention; 'I am here with full presence to witness and welcome my experience.' Pay attention to what unfolds in your body and mind with a kind curiosity, using your breath as an anchor. When you feel ready to finish, place your hand on your heart and say, 'Thank you. I love you. I accept you whole-heartedly'. Concluding with this gesture infuses your day with loving kindness that can radiate outwards towards others.

Key Qualities of Spring's Energy

ASSOCIATIONS
New beginnings, dawn, Air, east, new moon, maiden archetype, sowing, potential, planting, sprouting, birth, mental healing, mind, inspiration, vision, thoughts, ideas, conception, insight, imagination, knowledge, communication, sound, words, poetry, purification, pre-ovulation

CHARACTERISTICS
Childhood, innocence, joy, purity, wonder, curiosity, clarity, playfulness, renewal, regenerative, expansive, adventurous, open-minded, cleansing, growth, learning, exploring, optimism

COLOURS
Sky blue, green, yellow, whites, gold, pastels – pinks, pale yellows, spring greens, violet

FLOWERS AND PLANTS
Primrose, daffodil, bluebells, ramsons, cleavers, nettles, vervain, ash, alder, aspen, birch, beech, hawthorn

SYMBOLS
Fresh flowers, bird nests, eggs, budding branches, feathers, seeds, incense, books, pen, sword, clouds, basket, sky, chimes, wind instruments

ANIMALS
Hare, hawk, dragonfly, spider, blackbird, caterpillar

Cleansing With the Elements
Purifying mind, body, spirit and space

Before any ritual crafting it is important to prepare with a cleansing
process that supports you to release unhelpful energy so you can fully
inhabit your body, quieten your mind and open your heart to receive
the more subtle energies at play. Through this practice you also shift
your awareness, bringing your attention towards your ritual intention.

When I light a disc of charcoal in my ceramic bowl and hear it
sizzle, open my jar of herbs and offer some to the smouldering heat,
my senses awaken with the first wafts of sacred smoke and my whole
being knows I am crossing a threshold. I feel an alertness, a clarity,
and ancient memories stir of grandmothers using their crow feathers
to bathe me in cleansing herbal clouds. I can access these memories
because my busy thinking mind has been nudged out of the driver's
seat by the more intuitive, receptive awareness that arises from
practising rituals such as this that prepare me for entering sacred space.

This ritual process can be applied to cleansing the space you are
in, your home or work environment, or if you are creating a ritual
outdoors and want to ensure the energy is clear. You can also use
this ritual for a new moon energetic clearing or whenever you feel
off centre or notice your energy feels fragmented. There are so
many external and internal triggers that can intercept your sense of
connection with spirit, to your truth, especially if you work or interact
with lots of people on a regular basis and are picking up on their
energies. To cleanse at the beginning of a ritual, you can choose just
one of the elements to cleanse with.

INGREDIENTS

Smudge stick or herbs
and charcoal disc

Bowl of water

Candle and lighter

Feather

Musical instrument

Preparation – Open your windows if you are indoors and gather together everything you need before you start the ritual.

Grounding – Begin in stillness, lengthening your breath, expanding your awareness of your body as you invite your muscles to soften and mind to relax. Extend your breath down to your belly, slowly releasing the out-breath as you feel your body relax. Feel your feet on the earth. Visualise yourself as a tree with strong roots digging deep into the soil and rocks beneath, your body as a solid trunk with branches that spread towards the sky. Focus on this feeling of stability, being held by the earth and aligned with the sky.

Opening – Light your candle as you speak your intention to cleanse your mind, body, spirit and the space you are in, releasing any energy that does not serve you or does not belong to you. Welcome the Elements and any other powers you wish to be present and ask them to help with this purification. Your angels can be especially helpful when invited to assist with this ritual.

Air – Beginning with the Element of Air to help activate the energetic space, use your voice to make three long sounds, feeling the sounds vibrate through your body:

'OOOO-AAAAAHH-EEEEEE
EEEEEE-AAAAAHH-OOOO
OOOO-AAAAAHH-EEEEEE'

Using any musical instrument you have, hold it to your heart, inviting it to clear away any unwanted or stuck energy with the power of its sound. Drum, chime, rattle or ring as you move the instrument around your body until you feel an openness and resonance.

Fire – Light a smudge stick or charcoal disc, adding herbs or resin once smouldering; thank the spirit of the plant or tree for their purifying and cleansing properties. Blow on the embers to help the sacred smoke grow stronger as you connect with the purifying power of Fire. Hold the smudge stick in one hand, as you move it around your body from head to toe, under arms and feet, in between legs and around your head. Use a feather to direct the smoke, wafting it vigorously around your space, being sure to get into the corners of your room where energy can more easily get stuck.

Water – Dip your fingers into the bowl of spring water, giving thanks for the healing and cleansing qualities of Water. Flick the water droplets over your face, around the back of your head and neck, and all the way down your physical body and the energetic body that surrounds you. Use the water freely on parts of your body that call for her, wiping wet fingers across your forehead, eyelids or throat. Sprinkle water around the edges of your space and over any items or furniture you wish to be cleansed too.

Earth – Stand barefoot on the earth for three minutes, visualising all unwanted energy draining out through your feet into the soil to be recycled and support new life to grow. You can use your imagination and do this inside, but get outside when you can for deeper earthing.

The golden egg – Imagine a radiant, golden egg resting in your heart space that expands with each intentional out-breath, as though you are filling up a balloon. Allow the golden egg to grow bigger until it surrounds you, roughly 30cm (12 in) away from your body. Feel the qualities of this luminous golden energy infusing all your cells with vital life force and creating a protective shield around you.

From this clear and centred place, express your gratitude for the cleansing power of the Elements, and make a commitment to yourself – perhaps to be more discerning with your boundaries or to practise a daily grounding exercise. Give your body a good shake all over and jump up and down a few times. As you blow out your candle to finish, send this cleansing and purifying energy to those places and people that need it most at this time. Imagine that the wisps of smoke from your candle are carrying the blessings from your ritual out into the world and beyond, bringing balance to the Web of Life.

Home-warming
Blessing a new home and honouring the spirit of place

There are many traditions associated with moving into a new house that are believed to pave the way to a happy home. The term 'housewarming' comes from the age-old belief that lighting a fire in the hearth on your first night in a new home brings light into the dark, warding off unwanted spirits. A Russian-Jewish tradition is to bring bread and salt into the home before anything else, ensuring your life will be full of flavour and that you are always able to eat.

Buildings, like people, come with a lot of energetic baggage that tends to accumulate over time, so clearing out the old energy is a vital first step when arriving at a new space, even if you are staying for just a short while. Once the space is energetically clear, you can then work to welcome the qualities you wish to be present in your space, asking for the help of a deity associated with protecting the household. These were often fire goddesses, their altars set up near the hearth: Celtic Brighid, Greek Hestia, Roman Vesta, Norse Frigg, Lithuanian Gabija.

It is also important to acknowledge the spirit of place that accommodates your home, and the unseen and more-than-human beings that dwell there. Attending to these fundamental relationships will foster a deep sense of belonging and community, as well as cultivating balance by honouring the reciprocal nature of these relationships.

This ritual is popular with my clients, even those that have not recently moved but wish to deepen their connection with the place they inhabit or shift the energy when they feel some sense of stagnancy. It is also effective for harmonising a new workplace or setting up a community venue that you wish to bless for future gatherings.

Honouring the heart of the home – Open the windows and front door, and lay out your ingredients where you will need them. Decide upon the room you feel represents the heart of your home. Place your bowl of milk and seed there, and take three conscious breaths before chanting the heart chakra sound 'aaarr' to begin the ritual. Speak your intention to energetically clear and protect your home and bless the way ahead for a flourishing and peaceful home life. Welcome your spirit helpers and the Elements, asking for their assistance with clearing out the old and ushering in fresh, vital life energy.

Clearing out the old – See page 76 for how to energetically clear your home. I recommend using sage and rosemary for smudging, filling every corner with their purifying smoke as you move from floor to ceiling, downstairs to upstairs. Open cupboards and drawers to smudge inside. You may need to command any unwanted spirits to leave, stating, 'This is my space; I'd appreciate it if you leave now.' If you sense the energy is unwilling to leave, claim the space as safe and protected. Stamping your feet in spots that feel especially blocked, cold or damp can be helpful. You can also beat a drum, ring a bell, or whistle to enhance the flow of energy. When you have been through all the rooms, vigorously waft the smoke to the open front door to help all the old energy leave.

Threshold blessing – Sprinkle a line of salt in front of your front door, stating that all negative and unwanted energies cannot enter. Then trickle some water over the threshold as you ask for the spirit of Water to bless your home and all who enter. Place a few sprigs of rosemary either side of the door for protection, or plant or place a potted rosemary there for enduring protection.

Close the door and windows as you move through your home, visualising the spaces filled with bright and beneficent energy.

Welcome the new – Beside your bowl of milk and seed, light a candle (or fire if you have a hearth) as you welcome the protective energies of a deity you resonate with that is devoted to protecting the household, or the energy of love or harmony. I call upon Brighid, saying, 'I light this flame in Brighid's name. Join me here and lend me your ear', before sharing my wishes for a happy home life, being clear about qualities I wish to feel such as 'held', 'calm' and 'safe'. You might like to create a small altar dedicated to this deity in the heart of your home to feel their continual presence and attend to them with offerings in reciprocity for their protection.

Honouring the land – When you have filled up your home with these prayers, carry the bowl of milk and your seed outside to any spot where there is exposed earth – a crack in the pavement will do. Closing your eyes, feel the ground beneath you, holding you. Introduce yourself and explain that you are now living here and wish to be in right relationship with all your neighbours, seen and unseen. Acknowledge all those who have lived in this place and send them love. Ask the spirit of this place to accept the milk as a gift and thank them for welcoming you here. Pour the milk onto the earth and listen inwardly for any response you might receive.

Make a commitment – As a guardian of this place, it is now your responsibility to care for the land and other inhabitants sharing the space. Holding your seed in your hand, speak aloud a commitment of your intention to be of service – perhaps keeping the area free of litter, creating an outdoor altar for the nature spirits or planting seeds. Bury your seed as you let your commitment ripple outwards. When you go indoors, blow out your candle to complete the ritual or sit in front of the hearth and enjoy some 'housewarming'.

Ongoing ritual maintenance – Imagine the spirit of place as an elder who has much to share but also needs to be fed, respected and protected. Remember your commitment and show up to do it while also checking in about other ways you can nurture this relationship. In your home, you can hold regular clearing rituals with each new moon and stay attuned to subtle changes in energy that might need to be attended to.

Intention Bundle
New moon ritual to support manifesting your dreams

With each new moon, you are given the opportunity to reflect on what you wish to create and see manifest in your life and the world. From the moment the first sliver of the Moon appears until she becomes whole is a powerful portal for focusing your intention and committing to your vision by aligning with the natural forces of growth during the waxing moon phase. You can carry out this ritual when you are starting out with any new project or have a desire or prayer that you want to manifest in physical form.

This ritual is inspired by the despacho ceremony, originating from the Andean community of Q'ero, which was designed to petition the spirits for help by creating this beautiful offering to feed them.

Creating an intention bundle is a beautiful process that can be deeply personal or involve the whole family or community. Similar to a mandala, the bundle holds symbolic elements and the prayers of the participants. I often include them in sessions with clients who are at a crossroads in their life to help them focus their intention for the path ahead, and for those who are starting a new chapter after a divorce, redundancy or when their last child has left home.

I once worked with a family to weave together an intention bundle to help them find their new home, with the children bringing elements to represent all that they wished to be there. The items included a key, sweets, bark from a tree, ash from their hearth, apple cake, locks of hair and daisies! You can be as playful as you like with the objects you add, just so long as you are clear in what they represent for you, and that they are biodegradable whenever possible. Either use newspaper or natural fabric such as cotton, wool or hemp to wrap your bundle.

INGREDIENTS

Large newspaper
or natural fabric

Incense or herbs
for smudging

Charcoal disc

Lighter or matches

Objects that
represent aspects
of your intention
(such as seeds, herbs,
food, ash, flowers,
feather, drawings,
totems)

Natural cotton string

Spade

Water

Flowers, wildflower
seeds or birdseed

Preparation – Spend some time in the natural world, either walking or sitting quietly, to refine your intention for this ritual. Get clear on what you wish to create, imagining it already in existence and how you will feel once this seed has blossomed and fruited in your life. Consider the different objects you will use and what they represent. Gather them together before the ritual and have them laid out in your ritual space when you begin. Decide where you would like to bury your bundle within the earth.

Open sacred space – On the new moon, gather yourself by taking three conscious breaths into your heart space and light a smudge stick or add herbs to glowing charcoal to begin the ritual. Waft the smoke around you and the items for your bundle as you speak aloud your intention to create this bundle as an offering to life, to Gaia, in gratitude for the support and resources that are coming your way to manifest your vision in physical reality, according to the highest good. Welcome the spirit of the Moon, the directions and Elements, your guides and angels, and all whom you wish to be present, asking them to surround you with their love and inspiration.

Feeding the spirits – Open up and lay out your newspaper or fabric. Connect with your heart and the gratitude you feel from imagining this vision realised. Filling your chest with this quality of gratitude, visualising it as luminous, golden light, feel this beautiful energy flowing down your arms and into your hands.

Choose an item to begin with, stating what it represents and giving thanks for its generosity and inspiration, before blowing over the item and placing it on the paper, starting at the centre. Repeat for each item, arranging them intuitively as you appreciate the beauty and colour of this creation, keeping a steady flow of movement. Continue until you feel the bundle is complete.

Wrapping your bundle – Spend some time drinking in the fullness of your offerings, this prayer made visible. Trickle some water from the centre in a spiral outward to fertilise your intention. Pull in the corners of the newspaper or fabric one at a time, wrapping your bundle into a small square and secure with natural string.

Incubation – You might like to feed your bundle upon your altar with songs and prayers for the duration of the waxing moon, or dream with it next to your pillow, and then bury it on the full moon. Or you can go directly from the creation to the burial, keeping in ritual space with your heart open as you ask the Earth for permission to dig a hole for your bundle. Imagine you are drawing down the energy of the new moon from above as you pour water into the hole and lay down some flowers in gratitude for Gaia.

Place your bundle into the hole and cover it with earth, singing or sharing your thanks and praise to all those present as you do so. Scatter some wildflower seeds or birdseed over the area as you offer a blessing to the land and all the spirits that live there. Spend some time in present silence with the new moon by going for a night walk or sitting outside in the darkness. Ground yourself afterwards with a soothing cup of herbal tea.

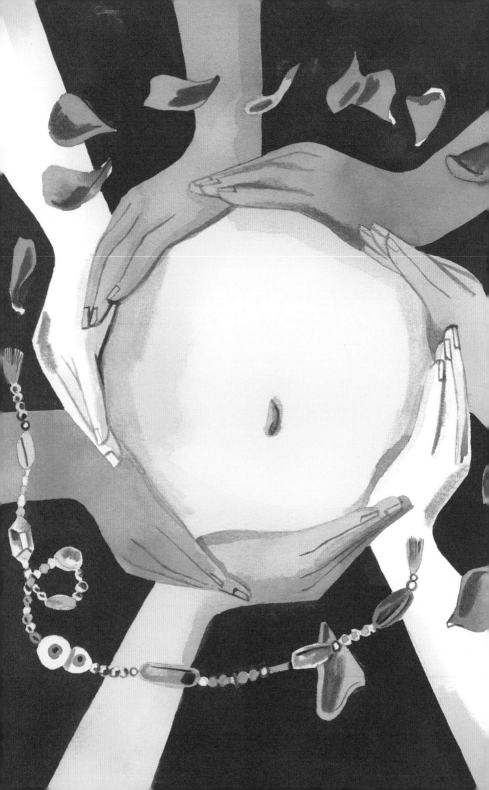

Blessing the Way
A woman's rite – honouring and empowering a woman through a significant transition

Women experience a number of significant transitions in their lives: passages of the body (menstruation, sexual initiation, childbirth, menopause, illness); passages of the self (marriages, birthdays, personal milestones); and passages of loss (break-ups, divorce, death). Each of these represents an ending and initiation into a new way of being that you can choose to consciously step into by creating a ritual to bless the way ahead. The inspiration for this ritual comes from one of the ancient Navajo healing ceremonies, the Blessingway – an elaborate and lengthy rite held for significant female transitions to invoke positive blessings and avert misfortune. These rites were designed to restore equilibrium to the Cosmos, and considered of vital importance to the wellbeing of the tribe.

As a woman, sister, daughter, mother and friend, I have felt deep grief for the absence of rites of passage ceremonies in our culture that recognise the power and wisdom of women and celebrate them as part of a sisterhood. When I first attended a version of a Blessingway for a pregnant friend, I was touched by the beauty and potential of crafting rituals to support and honour a woman at these transformative moments in her life. We massaged and bathed her feet, painted henna on her belly, fed her cake and fresh herbal tea, and heard stories from the elder women and mothers present about their experience of childbirth and motherhood. It felt like an ancient way of being together as women – sharing and weaving together in ceremony and celebrating our wild, cyclical nature across the threshold of death and rebirth.

I have also found this is a wonderful ritual to weave with a bride-to-be, to create a meaningful and sacred experience as part of a hen/bachelorette party, for a young girl that has had her menarche (first bleed), or for a significant birthday.

INGREDIENTS

Decorative items to
create a beautiful space

Altar cloth

Large bowl of water

Rose petals

Basket/box to hold
the letters

Red cotton thread
or string

Scissors

A chair suitable for
a throne

Massage oil

Flower crown

Items contributed by
the other women

Poem, songs, musical
instruments, playlist

Note – You can organise a Blessing the Way ceremony for yourself when you feel you need the support, asking a close friend to plan and oversee the proceedings. And be aware of women in your community that might not know of these ways and would benefit from a ritual that celebrates and honours how amazing, strong and powerful they are.

By gathering a support circle and blessing the way ahead, a web is woven of the most trusted and cherished women in your life, who can uphold you as you cross a threshold and integrate the changes. Partaking in these rituals supports the collective empowerment of women, reminding us of the deep well of wisdom within that is our birthright.

Preparation – Ask every woman to bring a bead, something to sit on, an item that represents the sacred feminine, a nourishing dish of food to share and a short letter of appreciation that might touch upon how they met the woman in transition (WIT) or a favourite story about her, accompanied with words of praise and gratitude that speak of her strengths and the gifts she brings to the world.

Choose a venue for the ritual that is comfortable and spacious – outside if the weather permits. Adorn the space with flowers, cushions, candles and colourful scarves, and create a beautiful throne for the WIT. Set up a central altar that holds the bowl of water and a bowl of rose petals, with space around for more items and a shallow basket or box to place the letters.

Invoking the goddess – With the women gathered in a circle around the altar, start singing, chanting or drumming as you welcome the WIT into the space and invite her to sit upon her throne. Open the ritual with an invocation to the goddess, asking her to guide and support the WIT through this transformation and inspire the ritual with beauty and love. Follow this with a collective sounding of 'Maaaaaaaaa' three times.

Greeting the grandmothers – Invite the WIT to stand and speak aloud her name and the name of her most recent three female ascendants – for example, 'My name is Susan. Daughter of Abigail, granddaughter of Caroline, great granddaughter of Rose' (or 'unknown' if they do not know their name) – as she scatters rose petals on the bowl of water in the centre and the women chant in unison, 'We see you, Susan'. Going around the circle, invite each woman to the centre to place her item that represents the sacred feminine upon the altar and put her letter in the basket, following with her name and three female ascendants, and a scattering of rose petals on the water as the other women say, 'We see you (name)'. Once everyone has spoken, share a minute of silence reflecting on the lineage of women that birthed each of you, feeling the power and support of this web of women.

Threading the necklace – Chant or sing a song together that lifts the energy and infuses the water with your love and appreciation. Pass a length of thread from woman to woman, inviting them to share a blessing or a quality they admire in the WIT as they string their bead on the thread to create a necklace. Focus on words that empower and celebrate the gifts of the WIT.

Adorning – With the necklace complete, secure it around the neck of the WIT with the intention that this necklace be a symbol of the support she has from this circle of women and all their female lineages, which can be worn whenever she wants to remember her power, her potential and her purpose. Celebrate with some singing or drumming, and then enjoy time pampering the WIT. Create a safe space for the WIT to share her fears and hopes for the future, if she wishes to. Bathe her feet in a herbal foot bath, allowing everything to be released into the water that might be holding her back from realising her full potential. Massage her body parts and adorn her with a flower crown, reminding her she is the sovereign of her life.

Activating – With all women standing, feet shoulder-width apart, placing their thumbs and index fingers in a downward triangle over their lower belly, breathe deeply all the way down to this triangle, activating this inner cauldron. Imagine a luminous, golden liquid held in the crucible of your hips. Start to circle your hips in a clockwise direction, stirring the creative elixir within your womb. Acknowledge this creative power and this sacred portal to the goddess that you can access at any time and ask for guidance. Invite the WIT to make a vow or commitment to herself from this connected place, imagining a seed being planted in her womb and activated by this creative energy.

Anointing – With the rose-petal water, anoint the womb, heart, throat and brow of the WIT as you speak a blessing for her journey ahead. Read a poem or share some inspiring words that celebrate the occasion. Pass the bowl of rose water around clockwise, so that each woman can anoint the sister to her left and offer a blessing.

Closing celebration – Invite the WIT into the centre of the circle as you make the collective sound of 'Maaaaaaaa' three times or sing together, allowing the vibrations to ripple through her. Give thanks to the goddess, your grandmothers and all present as you throw rose petals into the air before you move into more active celebration – dancing, drumming, singing – before sharing delicious food and drinks to help you ground. Before leaving, pour the remaining rose water onto the earth with a blessing from your hearts to all women everywhere, throughout time and space, that they may know and embody their power and wisdom.

Give the WIT the letters for her to take away and read whenever she needs reminding of her greatness and of the support available to her and encourage her to keep her necklace somewhere visible.

Variations

Depending on the rite of passage, you can create different ways of adorning the WIT such as body or nail painting, or dressing her in something beautiful such as a kimono or ceremonial shawl.

If you are honouring a pregnant woman, give each woman a candle to take away with her so that she can light it when the WIT goes into labour to recreate this circle of support.

This ritual can be adapted in so many ways. Ask the other women for their ideas and consider the needs and preferences of the WIT so that you can create something bespoke just for her.

Naming Ritual
Welcoming and grounding
someone in their name

Your name is much more than a label people call you; it's your unique
energy vibration that carries your essence, reverberating through
the Web of Life whenever it is spoken. It creates an umbrella under
which you live, and contains the seed-sound of your purpose, a key to
your gifts. Since you hear your name more than any other sound, it is
important that this sound empowers you along your journey.

In many traditions, names would change at certain transitions
in life, such as one's first hunt or after a vision quest. I experienced
a powerful naming ritual as part of the culmination of my shamanic
training, which involved my 20 initiated companions singing my
name and chanting the runes of my name over a period of time –
and after hours of sounding the others' names too – a feast of sound
and syllables, infused with tears and prayers as we marked the end
of our journey together.

Welcoming a new life and creating an intentional space to anchor
them into their name is one purpose of a naming ritual, but they
also serve to recognise someone who has changed their name with
marriage, chosen a different name or a spiritual name later in life,
as part of a transition of gender identity, and for those who just want
to reconnect with their birth name at a significant time in their life.
It is also helpful to craft a naming ritual for any new business or project
that has taken on a name as a way of launching it into the world on an
energetic level. I offer some suggestions for these variations at the
end of this ritual.

INGREDIENTS

Wisdom box

Three candles and lighter (lanterns or glass jars if outdoors)

Incense or herbs for smudging

Reading, song or poem

Bowl of spring water

Mud or red ochre

Feather

Tree sapling

Pots of bubbles

Acorns or envelopes of wildflower seeds

Offerings from the four guardians

Items for the wisdom box from the guests

Preparation – Consider who you would like to be a part of this celebration and send out invitations ahead of time. You will ideally have four people to call in as guardians – those friends or family members that hold some medicine or wisdom for the baby being named. Assign each one to a direction/Element and ask them to bring a reflection or reading that somehow speaks to the strength of that Element.

Ask the other guests to bring something to add to the wisdom box – some words, a poem, story, artwork or totem. Find a beautiful box or treasure chest that can be savoured for a long time to put these in.

Decide upon a melody for the soul song, or choose to freestyle on the day! Research what kind of tree you would like to plant. There may be an obvious choice, or you might consider a fruiting tree such as an apple, or a strong and long-lasting oak.

Choose a location that is intimate and comfortable, outdoors if possible. Consecrate the space before the ritual with a thorough cleansing with herbal smoke or sound. Create a simple altar at the centre of the space, with representations of the four Elements and three candles (in lanterns or glass jars if outdoors).

Welcoming – With everyone gathered around the altar, welcome them to the space and invite them to take three breaths together and make a collective sound such as 'aaaarrrr'. Share the intention for the ritual, acknowledge the spirits of place and call upon all guides and energies you wish to be present. Invite the parents of the child to each light a candle in honour of their lineages, naming them as they do so. Using the flames from both candles, they then light the third candle representing the life of the child and merging of their lineages.

Follow with an appropriate reading, poem or song.

Story of becoming – Invite the parents to share some personal reflections on the birth of their child and how their child's name came to them and what it represents.

Blessing with the Elements – Ask the four guardians to stand in the direction they represent, creating a circle around the child and parents. Starting with Fire in the south, invite the guardian to share their reflection or offering, concluding with a blessing with that Element upon the child:

FIRE/SOUTH: SMUDGE WITH HERBS OR INCENSE AROUND THE CHILD AND PARENTS
WATER/WEST: ANOINT THEIR BROW WITH WATER
EARTH/NORTH: PAINT DOTS OF MUD OR RED OCHRE ON THE PALMS OF HANDS AND SOLES OF FEET
AIR/EAST: USE A FEATHER TO GENTLY SWEEP ACROSS THE CHILD'S FACE AND BODY

Pronouncement – With the blessings of the Elements, the child is embraced within the circle of life and ready to be welcomed by their name. Pronounce them by their name in a way that is resonant for the child's family, for example:

'You are known by Mother Earth and all her creatures as (child's name).
This is your name, and it is powerful.
Bear your name with honour, remembering your soul song will always sing you home.'

Singing the soul home – Call upon everyone present to start singing the child's name, with the child at the centre of the circle of sound. Build the momentum gradually and keep singing for up to five minutes, until the space is humming with the child's name. Follow with a period of silence to let the vibrations settle. This is also a lovely moment to ask the younger guests to blow bubbles around the circle to send the soul song to the stars.

Tree pledges – Invite the child's parents and guardians to make a pledge to support and guide the child in some way and welcome any other guests to do so if they wish. If possible, plant a tree in the ground, or into a larger pot to take elsewhere to plant, with the parents and guardians each placing a handful of soil on the roots when they've made their pledge. Alternatively, they could donate to a tree-planting charity (See Resources, page 191).

Blessing the earth – Carry the child around the circle, stopping at each person so they can say 'Welcome (name)', and the parents can give each guest an acorn or envelopes of wildflower seeds to take away with them and plant with the intention of honouring what will grow in this child's life.

Closing – Conclude the ritual with a song or drumming and dancing to celebrate this new life, before thanking all those present, including the ancestors, angels and guides of the child, and the spirit of the place that held you through the ritual.

Box of wisdom – Before they leave, ask the guests to add their gift of wisdom to the special box. This box can be kept for a significant birthday, such as 13 or 18, to offer encouragement and inspiration as the child transitions to adolescence and adulthood.

As an alternative to the wisdom box, or if you are celebrating an older person taking a new name, you can invite the guests to bring a bead or charm to create a necklace that can help ground the person in their name. Each guest can thread their offering onto a thin cord as they share a blessing or wish for the person being named. Once complete it can be ceremonially placed over their head as their name is sung by the guests, and kept as a memento of the circle of support and good wishes available to them.

Variations

If you are naming a new business or project, it is important to consider the identity you wish to create and how the name looks and sounds. When you have landed on the perfect name, crafting a ritual to celebrate its birth is a wonderful way to support the business flourishing in the world.

You can print a poster of the business name or create a vision board with the name at the centre surrounded by images that reflect what your hopes and dreams are for your business. You can also imagine your business as an animated entity and draw or find an image or sculpture that reflects its personality or essence.

Once you have opened sacred space, begin by sharing your intention for your business and the inspiration for the chosen name. Bless this image with the Elements before pronouncing the name and sounding it aloud in a rhythmic way, to ripple these vibrations out into the world. Follow with planting a tree as you and your colleagues share your commitments for this venture.

Summer

The Dance of Summer

When the sweet, heady scent of elderflowers is wafting through my garden I know Midsummer is upon us and I welcome the invitation to celebrate the growth and fullness I see around me and feel within me. As the power of the Sun reaches its zenith in mid-June at the summer solstice, there is a building of energy and activity in the natural world as all life drinks in the light of the longer days. Vegetable patches are brimming with delicious salad leaves, broad beans, peas and the first crops of carrots and beetroot. Native woodlands are bursting with life, all the trees now in full leaf, creating a vibrant green canopy and sanctuary in the shade for those hotter summer days.

I love to witness the seasonal changes in my mother's garden, the different colours and textures, shapes and silhouettes that shift with the light of the Sun. At the height of summer, it's the roses that sing to me most, blooming their silky-soft petals in perfectly formed flowers that draw me in to sniff their sweet perfume. The grey stone walls all but disappear in the summer months as the climbing roses spread, the wisteria drips with bunches of delicate violet flowers, and fragrant honeysuckle weaves its way between rose and thorn, all alive with the buzzing of bees.

Ducking in and out from under the roof beams where their nests are hidden, swallow mothers work tirelessly to feed their hungry young, bringing worms and insects from the garden into their gaping mouths. In the field beyond the growing lambs delight in the abundance of grass, while farmers are busy cutting the surrounding fields to make hay before the rain comes. The pond that sits between fields is humming with activity as dragonflies emerge from the water and dart between reeds, water boatmen glide across the surface using their long, oarlike hind legs, and butterflies flutter between lilies.

In the early evening, the sun is still warm, and I can smell BBQ smoke mingling in the air with the assortment of floral scents that grow stronger as the day wanes. Sitting outside as the sun begins to sink, I love to watch bats as they dive and dance to the sound of chirring grasshoppers, and it seems like nothing is going to sleep!

The essence of summer

As you reach the lightest part of the year, with the solstice Sun beaming down his rays on the fields of grain and corn, swelling them to ripeness, the natural world is thriving and maturing. The creative powers are at their most dynamic, infusing your intentions and bringing daily miracles to life in the natural world as flowers bloom and beauty abounds. Through your hard work, resilience and commitment, your spring seeds have grown and are beginning to bear fruit, your visions manifesting into form. With all that is flourishing, you can celebrate the abundance in your life, give generously, and take more risks with new ventures as you feel better resourced and energised.

The warmer days and extended light feed your cells just like the plants, so that you feel greater strength, vitality and optimism. You are drawn outdoors to delight in the beauty and fullness of the natural world, to be among friends, socialising, mingling and making new connections. Physically you may feel an increase in stamina or ability to be more physically active in general. There is a maturing that comes from the shift from spring to summer: the maiden becomes the mother, nurturing and caring for others, multitasking and moving more energy than was thought possible. The mother archetype is also connected with the full moon, shining brightly in all her glory, tempting us to stay up late to bask in her fullness and dance until dawn.

With more outward focus, summer heightens your awareness of your sensory body and the ways you experience the outer world. Wearing fewer layers and exposing more of your skin, you become more intimate with nature, feeling the warmth of the sun on your face, the earth beneath your bare feet, the coolness of the shade beneath a majestic oak tree. You are more attuned to your sensual pleasure and what turns you on, attentive to your passion and the fire that dwells within you. There is immense creative power available to you when you connect with the fiery energy of summer and direct this energy towards what brings you joy. Fire is a powerful transformer, fast-moving and sometimes volatile, that can bring radical change and spiritual healing. At the peak of summer anything feels possible.

Ways to attune to the energy of summer

The invitation of summer is to create, express, dance, celebrate and gather in community, enjoying the beauty of the natural world and your sensual body. It is the time of year when I love to go on adventures with my son; bundling our tent, sleeping bags and stove into the car, setting off to explore sacred sites, find wild swimming spots, toast marshmallows on the fire and change the rhythm of our days to allow for more spontaneity and playfulness. I love sleeping on the earth, walking barefoot and bathing under the moon, becoming a part of the natural ecosystem and feeling the creative life force pulsing through me.

You can intentionally connect more with your senses during the summer months, enjoying what brings you pleasure and enlivens your body to replenish all the energy you are giving out. Through touch, play, dancing, listening to music, using essential oils or gathering aromatic plants and flowers, let your senses be fed by beauty to encourage your creativity to flourish. The expansive energy of summer supports you to try new things, explore innovative ideas and unknown places, and collaborate with others on projects and gatherings. If you have an idea for an event, take the first steps and contact someone you envisage working with to make it happen. There is so much vitality available at this time, you can fuel your passions with constructive action and manifest what you wish for.

As you witness the growth of your spring seeds and the mysterious ways your prayers are being answered, it is also the time for expressing your gratitude by feeding the Web of Life with your offerings, generosity and devotion. Through gatherings and ceremonies, you can share in celebration with others and delight in the beauty of summer. Picnics, camping and festivals are some of the ways you can enjoy the sociable summer portal and the feeling of expansion, connection and possibility.

Lots of plants and flowers are most potent during the summer as they drink in the sunlight, so now is the time to go foraging and gather what you need to see you through the colder months, as food and medicine. Elderflower cordial and champagne make delicious accompaniments to any BBQ or community feast. Medicinal plants such as valerian, yarrow, clover, plantain, self-heal and St. John's Wort can be gathered to dry for tea and making tinctures. I love to pick aromatic herbs such as sage and rosemary from my garden, adding them to a pot of honey to infuse, making a delicious medicine for keeping colds at bay throughout winter.

One of my favourite plants, *Artemisia*, also known as mugwort, is traditionally harvested on the full moon closest to the summer solstice, making it a wonderful annual ritual that has become a marker point for my foraging year. I wrap bundles of the leaves into smudge sticks and dry plenty for tea, offerings and gifts. Plants are at the peak of their expression, making them easier to observe, talk with and listen to. This can be as simple as gazing into a flower or regularly visiting a particular plant or tree, becoming more familiar with their ways of communicating, asking questions or for guidance, and journalling about what you experience.

Daily summer rituals

Dance your mood

Moving your body to express your feelings is a great way to shift and enliven your energy. Starting in stillness, with one hand on your heart and one on your belly, ask yourself 'what am I feeling?'. Listen and sense the quality and texture of your inner landscape as you take some deeper breaths, exhaling fully with a sigh. Play some music and move your body instinctively, shaking, dancing, stretching, as you allow the music to guide you. Let the energy build and ripple through you, until you feel a natural completion. Coming into stillness again, place one hand on your heart, the other on your belly. Feel the power of your heartbeat and give thanks to your body and the vital life energy that moves you.

Tending your flame

Assigning a candle to represent your sacred flame, a symbol of your life force and purpose, creates a visible image of the fire within you that requires your attention and stoking. Light this sacred flame every day, even if just for a few moments, to connect with the truth of what you are. As you stare into the flame, take some deep breaths, imagining the energy of the fire circulating around your body with your breath. Speak aloud your commitment:

'I vow to protect and nurture the sacred flame within me, to dance with the creative force of life. Guided by its light, I commit to express my truth and share my gifts with the world.'

Blow out the candle, with the intention to keep the fire burning within, thanking your sacred flame for its guidance and inspiration.

Aromatic touch

Give yourself five minutes each day to extend your self-care routine to include some loving touch of your body with a delicious blend of massage oils – you can make your own using a carrier oil such as almond mixed with some of your favourite scents. Connect with your heart, take a few deep belly breaths, and call upon your innate body wisdom to guide your hands in loving touch and massage. Pour oil on to your hands, rub them together to generate some heat, and blow kisses on to them, infusing them with your love. Make contact with your body gently and intentionally, listening and staying present with the sensations to enjoy the fullness of the experience, invoking feelings of appreciation and acceptance.

Daily doodle

An intentional daily doodle is a playful way to express your creativity and explore your spontaneous expression, strengthening these pathways for other projects and moments throughout your days. There is no expectation of a particular outcome, just dancing on the paper as you imagine the pencil as a receiver and transmitter of creative energy. Let your gaze soften and your perception expand as you allow your thoughts to wander. You can continue adding to the same doodle each day, or dedicate a book to your doodles and start a new one every time.

Key Qualities of Summer's Energy

ASSOCIATIONS
Noon/midday, Fire, south, full moon, mother archetype, passion, sensual pleasure, purpose, spiritual healing, abundance, courage, ripening, thriving, skilfulness, empowerment, initiation, commitment, community, light, teachers, ovulation

CHARACTERISTICS
Creativity, generosity, expansion, manifestation, enthusiasm, power, fullness, strength, resilience, transformation, nurturing, socialising, exuberance, taking risks, dynamism, celebration, action

COLOURS
Bright yellows, oranges, reds, blues, greens, rainbow spectrum

FLOWERS AND PLANTS
Hazel, apple, oak, elder, meadowsweet, St. John's Wort, yarrow, calendula, rose, lavender, mugwort, honeysuckle, dandelion, nettle

SYMBOLS
Fire, candles, flower crown, lamps, grains, grasses, dragons, summer produce of all kinds, flowers that are going to seed, chillies, spices, gold, maypole and ribbons, lightning, sun, stringed instruments

ANIMALS
Buzzard, kite, eagle, fox, mouse, bee, horse, snake, cricket, butterfly

Earth Mandala
Weaving with nature to celebrate creativity and growth and inspire collaboration

One of my most beloved rituals is creating mandalas as offerings for Gaia and the spirit of a place, or to honour a specific moment in time. The process involves opening up to creative inspiration and collaborating with the greatest artist of all – Nature – while creating something beautiful for the more-than-humans to feast upon!

A mandala, Sanskrit for 'circle', represents wholeness, harmony and unity. They have been used as meditation aids by Buddhist monks and created for devotional purposes in Islam and Celtic paganism. Creating one as a ritual provides an allegorical mirror in which the balance created in the mandala can reflect your inner state. When I hold a rite of passage ceremony for a client, I will often invite them to create a mandala to finish as a way of integrating their journey, helping them to embody their new state and anchor this sense of balance.

Gathering the flowers and foliage for your mandala in an intentional way is an essential part of the ritual. Firstly, ask permission from the plant or place in whatever way feels natural to you, and take heed of the response. Practising reciprocity by gifting something to the plant you harvest from and being mindful to only pick what is abundant and nearing the end of its growth cycle will ensure you are in right relationship with the plant spirits.

INGREDIENTS

Scissors or
secateurs

Basket

Offerings for
the plant spirits

An array of seasonal
flowers, leaves,
seeds and fruit

Small jug of
water

Preparation – Decide when and where you would like to create a mandala. Choose a route to walk and gather foliage that is likely to have an abundance of plants and natural objects, such as woodlands, parks, beaches and alongside hedgerows and wildflower verges. You can also add elements from your vegetable patch or kitchen for more variety and symbolism, such as lentils, eggs, rice and beans.

Gathering gifts – As you set out on a walk, basket and scissors in hand, take a few moments to feel your feet on the earth, the rhythm of your heart and breath. Speak your intention to gather gifts from the natural world to weave into a mandala as an offering or prayer. Ask to be guided to the plants and blooms that want to collaborate with you as you go forth, paying attention to your sensory body as you drink in the beauty of the world that surrounds you. Look out for fallen leaves, seeds and sticks or anything that is already provided. When you feel drawn to something, ask for permission to take them. Listen in and if you sense a 'yes' leave an offering of some sort – a song or a strand of hair will do nicely, or some birdseed or breadcrumbs. Continue walking with presence and gratitude through the landscape as you gather what you need for your mandala.

Preparing the ground – In the place where you wish to create your mandala, kneel on the earth with your gathered gifts next to you. Settle into the space by spending a few minutes in silence, listening and tuning in to the subtle energies and spirit of this place. Affirm your intention – to honour your journey, to celebrate a seasonal shift, to give thanks and pray – whatever is alive for you. Place both hands on the ground and speak your intention aloud. Bow your head to the earth and acknowledge Gaia, expressing your gratitude for her generosity, abundance and nourishment.

Weaving your mandala – Starting with a central point that represents you, place a single bloom or seed. Place one hand on your heart, the other on the earth and say, 'I Am because you Are', allowing the gratitude and love from your heart to spill over into your arms and hands, guiding you to add natural items outwards from this central point in whatever way is pleasing and intuitive for you. Let there be flow and continual motion. Stay connected with the frequency of love with each element you add, sharing your gratitude aloud for yourself at the centre, for your family and community, and the wider world and Web of Life as your mandala radiates outwards.

Blessing the blooms – Gently pour a stream of water over your mandala, starting from the centre and spiralling outwards in a clockwise direction. Imagine the life-giving waters activating your prayers, rippling blessings of love out into the world, healing imbalance and separation, and fertilising the seeds of your intention. Spend some time gazing at the mandala, inviting the beauty and harmony you have created to feed you. When you feel ready to finish, give thanks to the spirit of place and the generosity of the earth, and clap your hands three times over the mandala to close the ritual space.

Earth Vessel
A ritual to prepare you for
crossing your birthday threshold

The annual celebration of the day you were born is one of the most familiar rituals in modern times. This anniversary of your birth becomes an anchor point that carries you through each turn of the seasons and the solar year, providing an opportunity to reflect on all that has passed, acknowledge what you've learnt and sow dream-seeds for the future.

Gathering together with friends and enjoying a time of joviality and merriment is one way to mark the occasion, but I have found I am increasingly drawn to spending my birthday on a solo pilgrimage, walking in celebration of my life and taking the time to review the last year, stopping at pivotal moments to craft simple rituals of reciprocity with nature and, at some point, re-birthing myself with a wild swim or bathing at a natural spring. You can tap into this transformative energy of rebirth by choosing to consciously celebrate your birthday with a meaningful ritual.

Here you are invited to spend the evening before your birthday connecting with this transformative potential, using your hands and heart to shape and mould a bowl or pot made of clay, that you can ritually feed over the coming year and then return to the earth on the eve of your next birthday, when you repeat this ritual and make a new pot. Repeating this ritual each year creates a rhythm of resonance that your soul connects with in deep and mysterious ways and supports your crossing of the threshold into another year in an embodied and intentional way.

INGREDIENTS

Photo of you

Altar cloth

Items for your altar

Candle and lighter

Music

Incense or diffuser
and essential oils

Journal and pen

Ceramic bowl

Air dry clay

Newspaper

Pencil/toothpick

Water

Offerings for the Earth

Preparation – Gather items for your altar and clear the space, laying down a beautiful cloth in preparation for the ritual. Set up a space to mould your clay – you might want to lay down some newspaper. If you are repeating this ritual, choose a day close to your birthday to carry your vessel from the previous year to a place you feel drawn to in nature. Bury your vessel, leave it resting at the base of a tree, or offer it up to the spirit of Water – a river or the ocean. You might feel moved to smash it and let the seeds scatter. See this part of the ritual as letting go of the past year, clearing the way for a new beginning.

Birthday altar – Create an altar with a photo of you next to a candle at the centre, and arrange flowers and symbolic objects in an intuitive way. Put on a favourite playlist and add a delicious scent with incense or diffusing oils to create a sensual space. Light your candle as you speak aloud your intention to honour this threshold by releasing the past and opening up to receive the blessings of the coming year. Welcome in your guides, benevolent ancestors and all other energies you wish to be present to support you.

Reflect and release – Think back to your last birthday and what was happening in your life: what were you excited about? Who figured prominently? What were you working on? Respond to these questions in your journal; reflect on the challenges you met in the past year, the lessons learnt and insights gleaned. If there are aspects you want to let go of before starting another year, write them on a piece of paper. Gather your intention to release the past as you place the corner of the paper into the candle's flame and say aloud, 'With these flames I release and transform'. Hold it until it ignites, watching the words and their energy burn away, then place it in the ceramic bowl. Take a deep breath and exhale a loud sigh, shaking out your body.

Clay play – With the space this creates in your life, you can now vision the year ahead. Prepare a piece of clay – roughly the size of an orange – by warming it in your hands and beginning to work it between your palms. When it is pliable, start to shape it however you feel inspired to, with the purpose of making a vessel that can hold your seeds, such as a shallow bowl. As you work, conjure images of the year ahead in alignment with what you wish to experience during this next cycle around the Sun. Carve any symbols you feel drawn to on your vessel with a toothpick or pencil.

Goodnight, my love – When your vessel feels complete, choose a theme for the year that summarises what you wish to experience, such as 'trust', and carve the word onto the bottom of your vessel.

Holding your vessel, share what you appreciate about yourself. Be generous here, acknowledging your gifts and the challenges you have overcome, adding a seed to the vessel for each quality you praise. Give thanks to your guides and all who were present. Place your vessel on top of your photo on the altar and tap it three times as you say 'goodnight, my love', and blow out your candle to close the space. Enjoy a ritual bath or smudging yourself with smoke to help you ground and prepare for crossing your birthday threshold.

Birthday morning – Take your vessel outside and start by facing the east; holding your vessel up as you express your gratitude for the Elements and directions. Next give thanks to the Sun and Cosmos above and crouch down to the earth and bow your head to touch the ground, acknowledging the great Web of Life that supports you, giving thanks for this opportunity to grow a year older and be a part of this beautiful life. Scatter an offering of birdseed, water or herbs. Leave your vessel outside to be dried and warmed by the sun, if possible, otherwise on a windowsill.

Tending your vessel – Keep your vessel on your altar or a place in your bedroom that you will see regularly. Over the coming year, at significant moments and whenever you feel drawn to, hold your vessel and connect with the intention you carved into this clay. Add new intentions and prayers by speaking into your vessel and adding seeds or dried petals to fill its belly with your hopes and dreams.

Muse of Transformation
Full moon ritual to overcome challenges with creative play

In the portal of the full moon there is the invitation to look closely at your life, especially the more hidden aspects, by shining the bright and luminous light of the Moon into the shadows. Reflecting on what intentions you seeded at the new moon, you can consider whether there is anything holding you back or obstructing the growth of your dream-seeds. The full moon provides a peak of energy that highlights opposing polarities and forces in your life so you can see more clearly the dynamics at play.

Crafting ritual around this time imbues your life with the symbolic and energetic qualities of the full moon – the qualities of power, amplification, action – and an increase in subconscious activity that produces enhanced intuition and insight. By performing a full moon ritual, you are stepping into your personal power and actively petitioning and preparing your unconscious mind for transformation.

This ritual explores the idea of having a creative muse that can be called upon to inspire and support you through transformative processes. We are all artists in one way or another and the muse can help you embody yours more fully if you are willing to be curious, open and play with this notion. I suggest wearing a jazzy jacket to help you imagine this other aspect of yourself, but choose any garment that helps you connect with the qualities of mischief, magic and gaiety!

INGREDIENTS

Smudge stick
or herbs and
charcoal disc

Cloth and items
for your altar

Bowl of water

Candle and lighter

Incense

Poem or song

Paper

Pen or pencil

Watercolour/acrylic/
pastel paints

Jazzy jacket

Music

Create an altar for the Moon –
On the day of the full moon, dedicate
a space to your ritual, cleanse it with
herbal smoke and lay down a cloth.
Place a bowl of water at the centre,
and add objects and symbols that
represent the qualities of the Moon.
Include other items that inspire your
inner artist – an artwork you adore,
something you have crafted or a
symbol of what you want to create.

Opening – Light incense and a candle
as you welcome the spirit of the Moon
into your home. Dedicate a song
or poem to the Moon, lay out some
offerings for her on your altar and
sprinkle the objects with water.

Holding the bowl of water, speak aloud your intention to align with
the energies of the full moon and look deeply at what challenges you
are facing so that you may transform and release anything that is
holding you back. Welcome your guides and other supportive energies.

By the light of the Moon – Sit in front of your altar, or outside bathing
in the moonlight if possible. Feel the light of the Moon shining upon you,
infusing your cells with her luminous glow. Ask for her light to reveal
any beliefs or habits that are holding you back or stunting the growth
of your new moon seeds. Quietly reflect on the ways you might have
scattered your energy by saying 'yes' to everything, leaving yourself
drained. Is there a difficult conversation you have been avoiding?
Have you been distracting yourself from uncomfortable feelings with
too much screen time, alcohol or overeating? When you have a sense of
something you are ready to let go of, express your thanks to the Moon.

Articulating the challenge – Write down what you want to release. Try
to evoke how this challenge is making you feel by drawing expressively on
the paper. Once complete, place both hands flat on the paper and state
out loud, 'May the full moon help liberate me from this challenge.'

Welcoming your muse – Call forth your muse by standing in front of your altar and asking that they join you. Put on your jazzy jacket, sensing any shift in your being, and entice your muse through word and song. Play some music and shake out any tension or resistance.

Transforming – When you feel connected with your creative muse, choose some paints that evoke the feelings that you would like to experience going forward. For example, you may wish to step into your personal sovereignty and choose reds and oranges, or you might want greater calm and clarity, reflected in shades of blue. Using these colours, paint over your challenge as you collaborate with the creative powers of the Moon and muse that are alive in you. You may wish to paint a scene to represent yourself overcoming the challenge, or something abstract that feels bold and different.

Affirmation of gratitude – Looking at your picture, what is the essence of what you wish to feel through transforming your challenge? Joy? Clarity? Trust? Write out 'I am grateful for the _____ I feel in my life' using your chosen word and repeat out loud three times. Lay this affirmation on your altar.

Moon-bathing – Place your picture outside or on a windowsill, with the bowl of water from your altar on top, to drink in the moonlight and symbolically amplify your intentions. Close down your sacred space by blowing out your candle and giving thanks to the spirit of the Moon, your muse, and all those present during this ritual.

Drinking the Moon – The next morning, place the picture on your altar to keep your intention present. Repeat your affirmation three times and drink a sip of your moon-charged water. Sprinkle some around your home, repeating your affirmation. Repeat for the next three mornings.

Conclusion – Thereafter, you can clear your altar space and burn your picture, welcoming the transformative power of Fire as you watch the flames alchemise your creation. Continue to repeat your affirmation throughout your day until you naturally let it go.

Coming of Age
Celebrating the passage from childhood to adolescence

Societies all over the world across millennia have well-defined, often elaborate coming-of-age traditions. They usually involve lengthy preparations on the part of the initiate and the tribe, a challenge or ordeal that must be faced, followed by extensive ceremony and celebration with the community as the young people are welcomed back and integrated as a member of the village. These rites of passage form the basis for village life, ensuring the initiates become resourceful and valuable members of the community, sharing their gifts for the welfare of all.

Coming-of-age rituals in the modern, Western world are desperately lacking. Missing the opportunity to mark this threshold time in a ceremonial way fails our children, forcing them to initiate themselves – often in destructive or harmful ways. Providing a ritual container that supports the child as they take their first steps into adolescence encourages them to consider what it means to be an adult and what qualities are important to cultivate in order to live a full and authentic life.

A coming-of-age rite can empower a young one to consciously choose the path they want to take and help them recognise their worth and the gifts they have to share with the world. The key to a transformative rite of passage is helping the child to recognise their spiritual strength and how this relates to their vital role in the Earth community as they expand their sense of self – moving them from the 'me' to the 'we' as they begin to see their role and responsibility as part of the wider human and natural communities in which they are embedded.

INGREDIENTS

A community of elders

Natural offerings

5-litre container
of water

Fire-starting tools

Mud or body paint

Paper and pens

Drums and other
musical instruments

Note – It is beyond the scope of this book to describe the ideal conditions and extensive framework for a coming-of-age rite in the fullest sense, so I offer the following ritual as a starting point to mark the beginning of adolescence – around the ages of 10 to 13 – ideally to be followed with another rite when the young person is between 18 and 21. It is designed to cultivate wholeness by creating a challenge for each of the four directions and Elements, which you can easily adapt to better suit the individual child and your circumstances.

Preparation – Engage in conversation with the youngster about coming-of-age traditions and your wish to create something to honour them as they cross this threshold into adolescence. Help them prepare for the ritual by having discussions about this time of transition, going for days out with other influential adults in their life, and teaching them how to build a fire.

Contact some of the primary adults (elders) in the child's life – family members, teachers, sports coaches – and share your hope for this ritual, asking if they are willing to take an active role. Share ideas about possible tasks, locations for the ritual and what some of the gifts that they see in this child are, gifts that they want to celebrate and acknowledge. Ask them to consider what wisdom they would like to share with the child about this threshold time.

Invite other friends you want present to join for the celebratory part of the ritual. Plan to devote a whole day to this rite. Decide where the main part of the ritual will take place – somewhere that is safe to have a fire and has plenty of sticks – and what distance to make the walking with water task.

Greeting the day – On the dawn of the ritual, wake the youngster in celebratory spirit and take them outside to greet the directions, thank the Sun and lay an offering upon the Earth in gratitude for their life.

Share your intention for this ritual feast and welcome all the young one's guides, angels and benevolent ancestors to gather round to support and witness them on this special day.

If you need to travel to the next location, you might consider blindfolding the child for the journey to add to the element of surprise and adventure.

Carrying water, honouring life – Give the youngster the container of water without a lid and explain that they will be carrying this for their first challenge. To show them the responsibility of carrying life in their hands, they are to avoid spilling the water. Wave them off as they begin their journey, with two elders by their side who are not the child's parents; they are silent witnesses to the young one's journey, showing them the way and holding the space for this part of the ritual.

Arriving at a predetermined location, the youngster is greeted by the remaining elders and invited to pour water on patches of earth or roots of trees, as they symbolically let go of their childhood and prepare for new growth, thanking the water for her cleansing and renewal.

Gathering wood, sharing wisdom – One by one the elders go with the youngster to gather sticks to build a fire. This is an opportunity for each adult to spend five minutes sharing wisdom they wish they could go back and give their teenage self – this is a precious and powerful gift that helps to have been considered ahead of time. Imagine the sticks represent this wisdom that is being gathered, also acknowledging the wisdom of the trees where they come from.

Tending fire, celebrating gifts – With a generous pile of wood-wisdom gathered, invite the youngster to build a fire in a safe way, considering the other beings that dwell here. Provide them with the essentials and leave them to it, encouraging them to use the time with the fire to share anything that is troubling them.

After the youngster has spent a period of time alone with the flames, gather the elders around the fire in a circle and welcome the youngster's family and friends to join them by drumming or singing, as you celebrate the youngster's gift of fire.

Go around the circle inviting each person to share what they see the young one's gifts and strengths are, including the skills and character traits they have shown during the tasks for the ritual. As each person does so, they add a stick to the fire. It is worth recording these reflections on pieces of paper that can be kept in a jar or box and revisited when the youngster needs reminding of their gifts.

Speaking truth, the power of voice – Ask the youngster to share what three gifts *they* recognise in themselves. Invite them to make three commitments or intentions for the next phase of their journey, and express three things in their life they are grateful for. With drumming or chanting from the community, direct the child to walk clockwise around the fire three times and go to stand in a new position in the circle, at which moment everyone cheers and welcomes the arrival of this young one into adolescence.

Follow with hearty celebrations and blessings upon all the community, with a round of mud, ochre or face paint – adorning everyone present with a dot or streak on their face – thanking them for their presence.

Remembrance talisman – After putting out the fire and ensuring everything is left as it was before the ritual, ask the adolescent to look around for any natural objects that speak to them. It could be a rock, a shell, a pinecone; anything that comes from that place can act as a reminder of this day. Expressing their thanks to the spirit of Place, and all those present today, the adolescent makes an offering and takes away the object to keep as a talisman.

Reinforce this new chapter by agreeing on some new responsibilities and allowances, such as a sleepover at a friend's house, cooking a meal once a month or babysitting a younger sibling.

Variations

There are many ways you can approach the tasks to better fit your youngster and environment. The tasks need to be something that stretches them, that they can achieve and feel a sense of accomplishment. They could:

- Read a map
- Cook their favourite meal
- Choreograph a dance routine
- Change a tyre
- Build a den
- Redecorate their bedroom
- Fix or make something
- Go for a night walk
- Sleep under the stars

As an example, the youngster might want to update their bedroom to reflect their current interests and age. The task might be to carry the pot of paint from the shop and to sort out their belongings, giving to charity those items they no longer want. Their elders could take it in turns helping to paint their room with them, sharing their wisdom as they decorate, and writing in pencil hidden words of encouragement that can be painted over or concealed with pictures.

To celebrate their new room, the youngster could invite some friends for a sleepover, making a favourite meal that a parent has taught them in advance. The elders and other family and friends can also be invited to share in the celebration, coming together in a circle to express the strengths and gifts they see in the youngster, followed by the youngster speaking their truth, as already described in the ritual. A ribbon can be hung across the newly decorated bedroom door, which the youngster can ceremonially cut and cross the threshold as an adolescent.

Sacred Union
A ritual to deepen connection and commitment in preparation for a wedding ceremony

A sacred union ritual is all about celebrating love and commitment and honouring the fullness of what love is. The modern-day wedding comes with so many expectations and pressures that the essence of the union, love, can be overlooked as couples strive to plan the 'perfect' wedding. By making a clear intention to create a sacred celebration infused with meaning, a wedding becomes more than just a party, it becomes a ceremony of transformation that will support you across the threshold into married life.

By dedicating the time to craft a ritual before your wedding ceremony to come together as a couple and consider your intention, hopes and dreams, you create the space for deeper communication and truth to be shared, building a strong foundation for your marriage to grow from. It is also an opportunity to acknowledge the way your commitment to love is fed by, and feeding, the wider Earth community, expanding your sense of support and possibility.

Preparatory rites, crafted as a couple or with a small number of close friends ahead of your nuptials, will enrich your wedding day, infusing the ceremony with the potent expression of your unique love story. There are various aspects to this ritual, which can stand alone and also be included as part of ongoing relationship maintenance, whether or not you are married.

INGREDIENTS

Items for the altar

Smudge stick or herbs
and charcoal disc

Two candles and lighter

Paper and pens

Timing device

Washing-up bowl

Warm water

Epsom salts

Flannel and towel

Two sticks

Wool or thread

Scissors

Bowl

Two cups of water

Earth offerings

Preparation – Choose a day a week or so before your wedding to dedicate to this ritual and decide where you would like to hold it.

Go for a walk beforehand individually with the intention of finding a straight-ish stick that represents your commitment to your partner. Use the journey as an opportunity to reflect on what the commitment is that you will be making with your marriage.

As a couple, gather items for an altar that represent some of the qualities and aspects you wish to invoke for your marriage. Share your wishes for this ritual and settle on a mutual intention that will guide the way and write it down. Decide on a couple of key questions you would like to explore together, such as 'What do you hope for in this relationship?', 'What do you fear in this relationship?', 'Why are we getting married?'. Write these down too.

Creating sacred space – Enjoy time together setting up your altar, including the candles, cups of water, bowl, symbols for the Elements and the other items you have gathered, sharing what these items represent for you as you lay them down. Cleanse the ritual space with sacred smoke, taking it in turns to smudge one another from head to toe. As you both light a candle, read your intention aloud in unison and welcome the more-than-human helpers and guides you wish to be present to support this ritual.

Eye gazing – Sit cross-legged facing one another with your knees touching, or in a comfortable position where your eyes are level. Set a timer for 10 minutes. Take three deep breaths together as you settle into your bodies and invite your minds to settle. Look into the eyes of your partner, gazing softly, as you connect your energies without speaking.

Back-to-back – When the timer goes off, thank your partner and share a 10-second kiss as you place your hand on the other's heart. Turn around to sit back-to-back against each other, hold your stick in your hands and spend a minute in silence to settle into this new position, feeling the beauty of your heart connection.

Share your intention to speak and listen from the heart. Take it in turns to ask and respond to the questions you previously decided upon, giving time in silence between responses to let the words land. After you have both shared, turn around and look each other in the eye, acknowledging what you heard and what you spoke.

Cleanse with water – Prepare the washing-up bowl with warm water and Epsom salts for a footbath. Bathe your partner's feet, washing them with a flannel, as you ask for the cleansing waters to wash away any fears or emotional blocks to support your partner to embrace marriage with an open heart.

Dry their feet and invite your partner to vigorously throw away the water when they are ready to do so, releasing their fears and asking the Earth to recycle this energy for the highest good. Swap over so that you have your feet bathed by your partner and repeat the process.

Binding sticks, uniting dreams – Come together holding your sticks and speak anything that wishes to be spoken, including what you are grateful for about your partner and relationship. With your hearts full, hold your sticks parallel to one another and start to bind them together with thread or wool. Begin at opposite ends so you meet in the middle. You might like to weave in your dreams of your future together, imagining yourselves one, five, ten and fifty years from now and sharing your visions of what life could be like.

When the sticks are bound together, take it in turns to hold the bundle and feel the strength of this union. This bundle can be used as a talking piece for the times when you come together to consciously relate and share – something you might choose to do weekly or monthly going forward. In one year from now, create a sacred space together and explore the commitments you made, how you feel met in your relationship, what you are grateful for, and also express anything you are struggling with.

You might want to burn the original bundle and create a new one with revised commitments and updated dreams.

Weaving water, flowing together – Place the stick bundle on your altar. From feeling your strength together, you can now connect with the qualities of flexibility and receptivity that you wish to invoke. Pour the water from the cups into the bowl on your altar in unison, listening to the sound of water as it merges back together. Dip your fingers into the water and sprinkle or wipe it on your partner's face as you bless them with loving and encouraging words that express your support for their individual journey and your wish for their fulfilment. Swap over and repeat.

Libation to the four directions – Take your blended water outside and stand together facing east. Welcome the qualities and gifts of each of the Elements and directions as you ask for their support and inspiration going forward, speaking directly about how you would like them to help. For example, 'Air in the east, thank you for this sacred breath, the power of our words, clarity of mind and focus of intention. Guide us towards expressing ourselves faithfully to each other, sowing seeds of love with our words and thoughts. Help us to expand our perspective of what's possible in our relationship, be open to change and see each day with new eyes'.

Pour a libation of water on to the earth for each of the directions, feeling the power of the Great Web that is upholding you both on this journey of love.

Blow out your candle when you return inside to close the ritual, giving thanks for all the energies present. Enjoy a playful time together afterwards as you savour the connection and tenderness created from the ritual.

Daily earth tending – Every day after this ritual until your wedding ceremony (or beyond if you choose), go together and give an offering to the Earth that expresses your gratitude to the wider Earth community as they support and nourish your union. Scatter seeds or breadcrumbs, sing or dance, acknowledging the way your love feeds the Great Web and blesses life.

Variations

Creating sacred space for you and your partner to relate more deeply with one another is a vital part of nurturing and caring for your relationship. It can be a playful and sensual journey as you explore your edges together and learn to communicate more intentionally from the heart, listening to what is present and taking responsibility for your feelings. It's also important to find ways to communicate beyond words.

You can extend the above ritual, or try some of these other suggestions as part of your ongoing relationship caregiving:

- Draw portraits of each other
- Collaborate on a dance routine, poem or song
- Guide your partner blindfolded on a nature walk
- Write love letters to one another
- Design a ritual together that incorporates your interests and hobbies
- Create a time capsule, including meaningful items to seal in a box to open on a future anniversary

Consider incorporating some daily or weekly rituals that you can enjoy together as a couple, such as a morning tea ceremony and check-in, dancing as a way of expressing your emotions, or sharing your gratitude for the day before you go to bed.

Autumn

The Dance of Autumn

Each year my sense of wonder deepens when I go walking in deciduous woodlands in autumn and behold the treasure-trove of beauty, colour and abundance that nature gifts us. The light and warmth of the Sun has fed the trees and plants so generously they are now overflowing with nuts and ripe fruits. Shiny conkers, plump acorns and prickly beech nuts adorn the fresh carpet of brown, copper and yellow leaves that have fallen to the earth.

Treading carefully, I spot an array of camouflaged fungi emerging through the leaves, and those less hidden on tree trunks and mossy havens. My son and I love to venture to the forest with a basket, hunting knife, magnifying glass and identification book to see what species of fungi we can find, delighting in their unusual names, from octopus stinkhorn to dead man's fingers, collared earthstar to scarlet elf cup – and the rather sinister destroying angel mushroom!

We also enjoy gathering fallen nuts, seeds and colourful leaves to make into an earth mandala as a gesture of gratitude, creating beauty from nature's bounty and leaving a touch of magic for an unsuspecting walker to stumble across. When we sit to drink our flask of tea, I like to find somewhere near big swathes of mature ivy, one of the few plants flowering in autumn. We might just see the last of the bees and butterflies that are still gathering pollen from the yellow-green clusters of delicate blooms.

Where I live, I am surrounded by apple orchards that are brimming with fruit as autumn blows in, ready to be gathered and mashed into a sweet pulp and pressed for juice and cider. The hedgerows surrounding the orchards are dotted with ripe berries – sloes, rosehips, damsons, hawthorn, rowan, elder – a veritable feast for birds and humans alike. I love to walk around the fields nearby and fill up my basket with the fruits of summer, making the surplus into chutneys, crumbles, pickles, sauerkrauts and tonics to enrich our diet during the colder months when little else grows.

The essence of autumn

As the fullness of summer starts to wane, we begin our descent into autumn. Our past efforts are bearing fruit and we commence a period of harvesting and gathering, sharing the abundance with our community and giving thanks for all that has supported the growth of our seeds and creative projects. Once the nights begin to lengthen after the autumn equinox, we are lovingly called back inwards, to rest and retreat after the busyness of summer. We are gifted this time to reflect on what has grown in our lives and which of the seeds we are harvesting we wish to nurture and sow next spring.

The natural world gradually begins to wane as Earth surrenders her beauty to allow the decay of all that has reached the end of its growth. The Moon ebbs and wanes, supporting us to let go and clear away habits, beliefs and projects that are complete or no longer serving us. In the garden we harvest the last of our summer leaves and roots, cutting back dead foliage and offering it to the compost pile for transformation. The essence of autumn is release. You must enjoy and compost the fruits of your labours to make way for regeneration and renewal, creating space for new ideas and opportunities.

Midwifing death cultivates wisdom and an appreciation for life's mysteries, providing a training ground for becoming a true elder. You become an apprentice to grief as you witness the dying process within and around you, cultivating an intimacy with life that encourages the full breadth of emotion to be felt in all its bittersweet tenderness. The Element of Water is the guiding force of autumn, showing you the way to flow with your emotions and trust in the path unfolding ahead, surrendering to a deeper current within you.

Autumn is associated with intuition, healing and divination, as what you have learnt from your journey becomes integrated into wisdom. As the nights lengthen, there is a thinning of the veil between realms, making this a powerful time to communicate with your ancestors and guides in the invisible realms. With the autumn wind blowing you are invited to remember, to rejoice and give thanks for the myriad ways you are supported by life.

Ways to attune to the energy of autumn

There are two primary qualities of autumn that are interwoven and enriched by the other – giving thanks and letting go. Through recognition and celebration of all that you have in your life, you feel your basket overflowing and feel resourced enough to be generous and share your bounty with others. As you reflect on what you no longer need, let it go and grieve its passing, you create space and fertile conditions for new life to grow when the time is ripe. Your gratitude will feed your grief, and vice versa.

Spend time reflecting and writing about what has grown and blossomed in your life over the past year – the lessons learnt, the people that have supported and inspired you, the challenges you have overcome – to help you appreciate the fullness of your harvest. Surrounded by the fruits and bounty of the natural world you see the results of the growth cycle, the journey from seed to harvest, and the joy this brings. Gathering edible berries and medicinal plants, and learning ways to preserve and prepare them, reinforces your relationship with the natural world. My favourite healing elixir is a blend of elderberries, blackberries and rosehips brewed with rosemary, ginger, cinnamon and cloves and sweetened with honey – the perfect remedy for autumn's common cold and a powerful immunity booster.

As you spend time outdoors, focus your mind on gratitude and wonder. Allow yourself to bathe in nature's beauty and cool waters, going wild swimming or dipping your toes into a stream, feeling the movement of water and surrendering to the flow as you release.

With the dynamic energy of autumn in full flow, this is an empowering time to deep clean your house, body and mind. In your home, clear out clutter, smudge all the rooms and bless them with a sprinkling of spring water. Give your body a chance to reset with a fast from food, imbibing only green juices and lemon water, and enjoy a salty bath and exfoliation. This is a supportive time to commit to nourishing daily practices that will resource you through winter. Forms of meditation, movement, breathwork, journalling and prayer will all help carry you through the darkness, reducing the tendency towards depression and apathy.

As you begin to turn inwards, it is important to find ways to stay feeling connected. The festival of Samhain (end of October/beginning of November) provides an opportunity to honour and embrace your ancestors, offering your gratitude and asking for their guidance and protection. It is a time of remembering your belonging and who you are. Invite your family or friends to share a meal made up of foods that your ancestors enjoyed, offering a portion to the earth to ritually feed the dead. Create an ancestral altar with photographs of deceased relatives and items from the natural world to provide a focal point for your prayers. You can also visit graveyards and attend to the communal dead, clearing away any dead foliage around the headstones, trimming the grass, and wishing the dead well as you sing or recite poetry to them. You might be lucky enough to meet one of the many ancient yew trees that are often found in cemeteries – guardians of the dead and wise ancestors themselves.

Spending time in the company of trees during the autumn months provides the perfect example of how to release graciously as they so effortlessly shed their leaves to direct their energy down into their roots. As you sit with them, watching the wind carry their leaves to the ground, you can ask yourself, 'What do I need to support myself to let go of what's not working in my life and get comfortable with uncertainty?' You can draw upon the qualities of courage and resilience from the trees themselves, fortifying you for the journey ahead. The turning point of autumn is an opportunity to embrace a new set of possibilities and cultivate different ways of seeing.

Daily autumn rituals

Dream journal

Keep a journal beside your bed to record your dreams upon waking. They will become easier to recall with practice. It also helps to set the intention before going to sleep that you will remember them. Notice recurring themes or symbols and consider whether there are any messages or guidance for you to take heed of.

Cleansing with water

In the shower or bath, welcome the spirit of Water and ask that she helps wash away your worries and limiting beliefs, supporting you to release what does not serve you, including any dense energies or those picked up from other people. Feel how your body responds and softens. Imagine the water carrying away all unwanted or unhelpful energies, draining down the plughole to be recycled. Feel the water renewing your cells with vital life-force energy, filling you up with a diamond light from head to toe, surrounding your body as a protective field to uphold you throughout your day.

Giving thanks

Spend a couple of minutes when you wake up expressing what you are grateful for. Whether the warmth and comfort of your bed, the sound of birdsong or a conversation you had with a stranger that was an unexpected moment of connection. This is such a simple way to relate with your heart and expand your capacity to see and feel the many blessings in your life.

Blessing water

Infuse your drinking water with love and gratitude to welcome these qualities into your life. Hold your drinking bottle or a jug filled with water and chant, sing or pray with it so the loving vibrations penetrate the liquid. Write a word on the bottle or on a piece of paper for it to stand on, that speaks of joy, generosity and kindness. Drink throughout the day.

Release the day

At the end of your day when you are lying in bed, take a few minutes to give thanks for whatever lessons, inspiration and joy you received today. Consider anything you wish you could have done differently and then commit to letting it all go. You can imagine a waterfall washing down from your head to your toes and back to the earth, or that you are a tree shedding its leaves. Welcome a sense of feeling lighter and freer, before sinking to sleep.

Key Qualities of Autumn's Energy

ASSOCIATIONS
Sunset, west, waning moon, Water, wise woman archetype, gathering and harvesting, feelings, emotional healing, grief, gratitude, dreams, reflection, subconscious, intuition, prosperity, transition, maturity, relatedness, premenstrual phase

CHARACTERISTICS
Remembering, trust, release, letting go, surrendering, generosity, receptivity, flow, appreciation, compassion, discipline, healing, cleansing, empathy, intimacy, going inwards, slowing down, illusion, fear

COLOURS
Soft reds, orange, browns, golden yellows, blues and silvers

FLOWERS AND PLANTS
Wheat, barley, grasses, seed pods of all kinds, fungi, blackthorn, elder, yew, apple, willow, juniper, sea buckthorn, lotus, water lilies

SYMBOLS
Cup/chalice, cauldron, wells and springs, autumn leaves, pinecones, acorns, garden produce, corn, loaf of bread, harvested herbs, apples, pumpkins, shells, water-smoothed stones, rosehips, berries, cymbals/bells

ANIMALS
Owl, salmon, snake, whale, heron, bat, frog, otter, seal, turtle

Clearing the Way
Overcoming obstacles and embodying your sovereignty

Ritual 1

There can be times in life when things don't seem to go your way; you might feel a victim and are perpetuating unhelpful patterns that undermine your vision and goals, doubting yourself, being overly critical or avoiding challenges. Perhaps you are struggling with obstacles that are preventing you from manifesting something – a new job, house or partner, or committing to a wellness routine. Your inner power feels scattered and you feel pulled in different directions.

This ritual works on clearing away these obstacles with the purifying power of Water, creating the space for some intentional crafting that will help you to align with your power in an embodied way. A medicine bag or sacred pouch is found in indigenous traditions across the world; it is popular in Native American lineages, and known elsewhere as a 'crane bag' in Celtic druidry and 'mojo bag' in Afro-Caribbean cultures. These sacred pouches contain objects of power that offer protection and help clear away negativity. They can be a focal point for healing, enhance intuition and strengthen your commitment to your purpose. Inside, you place items that are meaningful to you that can be added to over time, representing qualities you wish to embody or that connect you with a place or time that you associate certain feelings with.

Your pouch can be made from any material and decorated in any way you choose. There is no one 'right' way to create one, and it does not need to be elaborate or even neat, so find your joy in this creative process, revelling in the journey rather than striving for perfection.

INGREDIENTS

Lemongrass
essential oil

Candle and lighter

Bath or
washing-up bowl

Epsom salts

Length of leather
or strap

Fabric/leather

Scissors

Adornments

Items of power for
your pouch

Preparation – Gather the materials you need for your pouch, including the items of power you wish to put inside; these may be natural objects such as an acorn or pebble, a piece of jewellery, a bead, or a mantra written on a small piece of paper. Consider what qualities you want to invoke and reflect upon what each item represents for you. Create a beautiful space to craft in when you have finished your bath. If you don't have a bath, make a footbath using a washing-up bowl and follow the same process.

Shedding the first layer – Prepare a hot bath with a cup of salt dissolved in the water. Add a few drops of lemongrass essential oil, a powerful cleanser of energy. Light your candle and speak aloud your intention to release all that no longer serves you, does not belong to you, or is obstructing your path so that you may embody your sovereignty and power. Call upon your guides and spirit helpers. Shed your clothes intentionally, as an act of letting go.

Surrendering to water – Ask the spirits of Water and salt to cleanse you and draw out all negativity and unhelpful thoughts and emotions. Gently immerse yourself in the bath, inviting your body to soften and open as you receive the healing blessings of Water. Take deeper breaths, releasing any tension in your body as you exhale. Speak aloud what is troubling you and identify the obstacles you feel are preventing your full, authentic expression. Be honest about your inner reality and those people, things or situations that are holding you back. Imagine your words rippling through the water as you give over these limiting beliefs, so they may be transformed.

Release – When you feel ready, take out the plug. Feel the water being drawn out as you imagine all you have let go of draining away, being recycled and transmuted in accordance with the highest good.

Stay in the bath until all the water has disappeared, using the time to express your gratitude for Water's cleansing power. Notice how much clearer and lighter your body feels.

Calling back your power – Carry your candle to your crafting space and stand tall – naked, or with a bathrobe wrapped around you. Gaze into the flame to settle your energy before closing your eyes and focusing your attention on your belly, this creative cauldron and place of power. Place your hands on your belly and imagine a sacred flame burning within that is filling your body with warm, golden light. As you feel your power stirring, raise your arms in a V-shape above your head, take some deep, intentional breaths, and speak aloud, demanding that all parts of yourself return to you. Welcome back the fullness of your power, allowing your body to move or sound in whatever way it wants to.

Crafting your pouch – With all this energy alive in you, focus your power into your hands. Cut two pieces of fabric into rectangles of the same width, but one with a longer length to fold over the top. Face the front sides of both pieces of fabric together and sew the three edges, leaving the top section free to form an opening. Turn it inside out and decide whether to create a buttonhole and add a button to hold the contents securely in the bag. Add a strap by making two small holes at either side of the flap, insert the cord and knot them to secure in place. Decorate however you wish.

Consolidation and coronation – When your pouch feels complete, kiss it and imbue it with your love. One by one, place your objects of power into it as though you are adding ingredients to a magical brew, holding each one before placing it inside and infusing your intention into them: what qualities do you wish to embody? What supports you to stay in your sovereignty? Place the strap around your neck with a sense of ceremony at this coronation of your power. Hold your pouch to your heart and make a commitment to yourself to embody your power and be a force for good – to protect what you love and share your gifts freely. Express your gratitude as you blow out the candle to conclude your ritual, imagining the smoke carrying the blessings of balanced power out into the world.

Cutting Ties
Divorce or separation ritual
to cultivate acceptance and forgiveness

After the ending of a relationship it can often feel like there is an emptiness in your life, as though something is missing. This is usually accompanied by recurrent thoughts and memories about your past love and times you spent together. It can become difficult to imagine beyond these feelings and thoughts, or you may tend towards distracting yourself to avoid any discomfort, so these natural feelings get suppressed, creating unhelpful patterns around relationships and loss in the future.

Intimate relationships can create an entanglement with the other person in our energy field that does not disappear once the relationship ends, so it is important to intentionally cut ties on an energetic level to ensure a healthy and clear break. This ritual will support you in this process of letting go of anything that does not belong to you and reclaiming what is rightfully yours so that you are free to move forward and enter into another relationship if you so wish. It is inspired by a ritual in William Ayot's wonderful book, *Re-enchanting the Forest: Meaningful Ritual in a Secular World.*

Through the process of cutting the ties you will explore what served you in the relationship – those things you are grateful for and wish to cultivate more of in your life – and express what you found difficult and hurtful, so that you can begin to accept and forgive what has unfolded and the person you are cutting ties with. Without forgiveness you continue to harbour feelings that drain your energy and prevent you from taking responsibility for your actions and how the relationship deteriorated. This can be an uncomfortable process, but it will empower you to make different choices in the future that lead to greater harmony and authentic communication in your relationships.

Preparation – Choose a place outdoors, on a patch of earth where you won't be disturbed. Take an old sheet that was used on your bed with your ex-partner, and cut a dozen or so incisions along one hem. An item of clothing, fabric, photograph or piece of paper that is reminiscent of your ex-partner will also suffice. Find an object that represents your relationship – something you were gifted from your ex-partner or an item that you feel carries some memories of your time together. You will need to let this go as part of the ritual.

Creating a safe container – In the place of your choosing, open ritual space by welcoming the directions and Elements, the spirit of place, and all those invisible helpers you wish to be present. Pour water onto your hands and face as you call upon yourself to be fully present. With your hands on the earth, state your intention to cut the ties with your ex-partner, returning all of their energy back to them and welcoming back all energy that is rightfully yours. After asking permission from the earth, dig a foot-deep hole in the soil.

Cutting the ties that bind – Tear your bed sheet into two pieces. Holding one of the pieces, say aloud what you loved and appreciated about this relationship, tearing along the incisions you made as you acknowledge each thing you are grateful for. As each strip comes free, put it into the hole in front of you.

With the other half of the sheet, repeat this process of tearing and placing the strips in the hole as you now express what was hard, painful and disempowering about the relationship. What do you want to let go of, change or end? With each tear let the sound of the ripping course through you as you feel these ties being broken and allow the deeper emotions of anger and hurt to come forth, bellowing sounds or words into the hole to help these be expressed.

Speaking your truth – Hold the token object from your relationship and imagine this is a representative of the person you want to cut ties with. Now is your chance to speak anything to them that feels unspoken, allowing your words and emotions to flow uncensored. You might choose to break this object using whatever will help you to do this, or even burn it, depending on the material. Place the object or pieces into the hole with the strips of sheet as you say, 'I return all energy that belongs to you'. Give yourself some time here to process your feelings, moving your body, sounding or lying on the earth.

Articulating the vision – Sit with your back against a tree if possible and write a letter to yourself that is a statement of love and appreciation. Describe how you want your future to look and feel now you have cut these ties. What are you inviting in? What would you like to do with the energy that was tied up in this situation? Let this be a joyful and exciting imagining including what you most want to do, be and enjoy.

Igniting the future – Holding your letter above the hole in the earth, light the corner of the paper and watch your loving intentions for the future be ignited by the power of fire, letting it go into the hole before the flames reach your fingers. With the smouldering paper in the hole, say, 'I welcome back all energy that belongs to me. The way ahead is clear and full of love.'

Cover the hole with soil, giving thanks to the Elements of Earth and Fire for their healing and transformative power, and to all those guiding energies present that supported you throughout this ritual.

Blessing your heart – Holding some rose petals in your hand close to your heart, express your gratitude to yourself and your courageous heart for taking this step of cutting the ties that bind and creating space for more love to come into your life. Scatter the petals on the soil over the place of your hole as you offer up a blessing to all beings who are tending a broken heart, sending them your good wishes and prayers of healing. Pour some water over the petals to close the ritual, and enjoy a few bites of delicious chocolate or another edible treat to help you ground.

My Body as a Temple
Accepting physical changes
and cultivating self-love

The pressure to look a certain way and meet the warped ideals of a society entrenched in false notions of beauty and meaning can deeply affect our own sense of worth and acceptance. I had hoped I would embrace the first grey hairs and wrinkles that started appearing with vigour after my son was born; I love looking at the stories etched on elders' faces that speak of their life and loves, but I fell into the trap of judging myself, feeling I wasn't ready to 'grow old', that it was somehow premature for these physical changes to be taking place.

I saw where this was going, so I committed to exploring my ideas of beauty and worked at reframing my self-image to accept the natural changes of my body and appearance. In conversation with friends, I found most of them shared similar concerns about the ways their bodies were ageing, cultivating a subtle resentment or rejection of themselves.

This ritual was born from these conversations and my wish to change my relationship with my body and the ageing process. It has been shared with others that experience different forms of body dysmorphia, including those struggling with eating disorders, body shame and people that have had some form of surgery or an accident that has changed their body in some way. My prayer with this ritual is to support you in coming home to yourself, in gratitude and wonder for the miracle of your body, your earth temple.

When you reject a part of your physical self you deepen the sense of separation at the root of all suffering. You are also rejecting the Earth of you; the natural, wild, innately wise and powerful physical being that you are. By re-enchanting your relationship with your body, you will begin a love affair that opens your heart to embrace the perfectly imperfect and evolving parts of yourself with appreciation for the natural cycles and changes you go through.

INGREDIENTS

Washing-up bowl or container for footbath

Essential oils (lavender, geranium, lemongrass)

Massage oil

Towel

Paper, pen and envelope

Rose water or rose essential oil

Hand mirror

Music

Blanket/shawl

Honey or maple syrup

Connecting with your heart – Create a sanctuary in your home, somewhere you will not be disturbed. Light a candle to open sacred space as you state your intention to reframe your relationship with your physical body and cultivate radical self-love. Breathe into your heart space, expanding your chest as you imagine pink light radiating outwards from your heart, filling your whole body.

Releasing the illusions – Prepare yourself a warm footbath with essential oils, get comfortable and place your feet in the healing waters. Call to mind any thoughts and feelings you have towards your body that are *not* rooted in kindness and love; speak them out loud. Notice how hearing them spoken makes you feel. Imagine these thoughts and words draining out of your body through your feet and into the water, allowing any tears or emotions to surface that want to be released.

After roughly 15 minutes remove your feet from the footbath and dry them. Take the water outside, gather your intention to let go of these illusions of self, stating aloud that you release and cast away these beliefs, and throw the water upon the earth with assertiveness, making any sounds that feel good. Cast the water down the drain with the same intention if doing this outside is not possible.

Seeing with new eyes – Returning to your sanctuary, undress and hold your mirror up to your face. Looking into your eyes, say aloud, 'I look upon you with the eyes of love'. Intuitively move the mirror around your body to those parts of yourself that you have criticised, lingering there as you consider their wisdom and beauty and speak kind words to them. When you have looked upon yourself fully, blow some kisses on to your hands and begin to lovingly touch and massage your body with oil as you continue to thank her for her natural intelligence and adaptability and for being a sacred vessel for you to live an embodied life.

Dancing yourself free – When your body feels well-tended, honoured and filled up with love, play a piece of music that beckons you to dance. Celebrating your nakedness, move your body in whatever way feels good and allow your inner radiance to shine.

A love letter to self – Come into stillness and drape a blanket or shawl around your shoulders, imagining yourself being wrapped up with love. Call forth your wise, elder self, imagining yourself at a ripe old age, living your best life, at peace with yourself. As you pick up your pen, ask for your elder self to write this love letter to you now, to share their wisdom and whatever is helpful for you to know at this time. Allow the words to be written spontaneously, without pause for thought. When you have finished, thank this part of you for showing up and sharing these words as you splash a few dots of rose essential oil or spray rose water on to the paper.

Honey for the heart – In front of a mirror, gaze into your eyes for a couple of minutes, noticing any feelings that arise. Read the letter aloud, looking up from time to time to see your reflection. Let the words sink into your cells. When you have finished, place a spoonful of delicious honey or syrup on your tongue, letting it slowly melt as you allow the sweetness of these loving words to permeate your being. With your hand on your heart, make a commitment to lovingly tend this relationship with your body and the Earth, so that the future generations will be free from this illusion of separateness and unworthiness, and receive the blessings of your love towards yourself.

Closing the container – Blow out your candle to complete this ritual, thanking all those present that supported and guided you. Place your letter in an envelope and keep it in a special place so that you can return to read it whenever you need reminding of your beauty and worth.

Tending the Well
Ritual to support the grieving process

There are so many textures and faces of grief, as there are boundless ways that grief can show up in your life: the death of someone you cared for; the end to a way of life, habit or relationship; the denial of a part of yourself that stirs in the darkness, creating an echo of loss that follows you like a shadow; the tides of ecological and ancestral grief that can be felt on a subtle cellular level or like crashing waves that force you to your knees so that the vast ocean of our collective grief absorbs your tears.

Over the years of holding grief rituals, I have witnessed the extraordinary capacity we have to hold the depths of our grief, the fullness of our love, the power of feeling fully and allowing that raw emotional energy to have its way with you, to be encouraged to move through you, transforming your sorrow to the sweetest praise for this gift of being alive. As we close each ritual, usually singing together around a bowl of water and tears, the shift in people's energy from when they arrived is palpable. Their eyes are bright and sparkling, hearts open and connected, and there is a softness in their bodies that blurs their edges and dissolves feelings of separation.

This rite is adapted from these rituals, with the image of the well serving to remind you of the deep emotional waters you carry within you that need tending to, so that they do not become stagnant, creating blockages, illness and depression. Unexpressed grief will search for a way out, bursting forth unexpectedly or quietly gnawing away as you make attempts to divert your attention, finding sanctuary in addictions that disconnect you from your authentic self. Regular grief tending can ensure a fluidity and movement that brings greater ease and balance to your life. You might like to expand this ritual to include a circle of others, taking it in turns to voice your grief and witness one another through this sacred act of grieving.

INGREDIENTS

Drum, rattle or your voice

Smudge stick or herbs and charcoal disc

Shawl or blanket

Bowl of water

A stone

Candle and lighter

Grief object

Music

Preparation – Choose a place that cultivates feelings of trust and openness, which feels safe for your feelings to arise and where you won't be interrupted. Prepare the space by using sound to clear the energy, a drum, rattle or your voice. Lay out a simple altar that includes your candle and grief object – something that speaks to what you are grieving. This could be a symbol of grief, such as an item from nature, or something that represents a specific focus of your grief, perhaps a photo of an ex-partner or a deceased loved one. In front of this, place your bowl of water and stone, and arrange some cushions or a blanket to sit upon.

Opening the ritual container – Once you feel the space is clear, take deep breaths into your belly. Feel your connection with the earth through your feet and the depth of your roots. Acknowledge how you are held up and nourished every moment by the earth. From this grounded place, breathe into your heart space three times, imagine it filling with a golden light as you speak your intention aloud and light the candle on your altar. This might include:

'May I feel safe in this space to attend to and express my grief, bringing healing to my heart, peace to my thoughts and appreciation for the fullness of life's expression. I ask the spirit of Water to guide me, to show me how to trust and let go, cleanse and renew myself.'

Welcome all those guides and energies you wish to be present, asking for their protection and holding for the duration of this ritual.

Connecting with memories of loss – Play a soulful, instrumental playlist if you wish. Get comfortable and pick up the grief object from your altar. Use your senses to connect with this object, inviting your grief to the surface. Placing your object back on the altar, pick up the stone, close your eyes and pay attention to the physical sensations in your body. Using the stone, touch those places that feel tender, contracted, painful, or in any way connected with your sense of grief or memories of loss. Rub the stone gently on your skin or circle it around the area, imagining the stone absorbing your grief and any other emotions, softening these places in your body and encouraging the energy to move. Take your time here, tending to your physical body and all those places where memories of loss have been stored. Sing or speak these words aloud nine times:

'I feel safe here. I know peace here.
I am held here. I know love here.'

Voice your grief – Kneel beside the bowl of water and place your shawl or blanket around you. Offer up words and sounds that express your grief. These can be words describing how you feel, your sorrows, or what you have lost, or you might want to shout your rage, lament, wail, whisper, sob – welcome it all.

Feed the waters – When you feel a sense of calm return, place your stone into the bowl of water as you let go and offer up your grief to the water. The stone is cleansed by the purifying Element of Water and can be re-used for this ritual purpose, or you might like to offer it to a waterway nearby. Hold the bowl or lean close to the water and share anything that you are grateful for at this moment. Consider what gifts have come from your grief, what lessons you have learnt, your courage and vulnerability, your beautiful, tender heart. Hug and thank yourself. You might feel inspired to sing a song to the Water too, thanking her for her healing and restorative qualities.

Closing the space – Smudge yourself from head to toe with sacred smoke, letting the remnants of grief gently fall away. Imagine golden liquid pouring down your body, cleansing every cell and infusing them with vital life-force nectar. Feel the golden light radiating from your body, surrounding you in a bubble of liquid gold, protecting you. If you feel like it, play a song that gets you dancing to fill yourself up with positive energy. Blow out the candle to close the ritual.

Feed the earth – Take the water from your bowl and pour it on to the earth, the roots of a tree, or a houseplant in your home. Visualise all the love you expressed through your grieving rippling out into the earth, through the networks of mycelium, blessing all life.

Tending the Roots
Feeding your ancestors, nourishing your roots

In many cultural and spiritual traditions around the world the ritual tending and feeding of ancestors is a vital part of their ceremonial life. The Mexican Day of the Dead, Japanese Obon, Fèt Gede in Haiti, and the original inspiration for the festival of Halloween – Celtic Samhain – are some examples of the rich landscape of ritual that honour our ancestors.

Many of these traditions incorporate visiting cemeteries to attend to the graves of their kin, making offerings, spending time with the dead, in silence and celebration, honouring those who have gone before by sharing stories and songs to keep their memory alive and ensure the balance of energy between the living and the dead and harmony within the Web of Life.

Family relationships are complex, and it can be challenging for people to make connections with their more recent ancestors if there are uncomfortable emotions associated with them, or if they have been adopted. There are also those ancestors who are not well or wise, who should not be engaged with. With this ritual I suggest you go way back over one hundred generations, to those healthy ancestors that knew how to live in a reciprocal relationship with Gaia. Here you connect with the more essential nature and archetypal energy of your ancestors in a safe way.

This ritual is intended to support you to create a practice of attending to your ancestors, to cultivate connection in ways that can be deeply healing and transformative. There is so much scope for re-enchanting our relationship with our ancestors, and I hope this provides a starting point. May this mark the beginning of a vibrant and auspicious relationship between you and your kin.

INGREDIENTS

Objects for your altar and tree temple

Candle and lighter

Smudge stick (rosemary/mugwort)

Drum or rattle

Eight stones

Bowl of water

Salt

Rosemary

Offerings (food, alcohol, seeds)

Preparation – Gather your eight stones by visiting a natural place and asking for guidance to help find your council of elders. Offer something special to the spirit of this place as you ask permission to take these stones home with you.

Create an ancestral altar in your home that includes photos of your family or landscapes where they lived, heirlooms, or items from nature that help to connect you with your sense of lineage and belonging. Add your eight stones to the altar, placing them however you wish to.

Prepare some offerings for your ancestors, imagining you are feeding them with things they love. Whiskey and oats are popular choices for my Scottish kin!

Choose where you will create a tree temple, preferably near to where you live so that you can visit often.

Opening the gateway – Stand or kneel in front of your ancestral altar, take some deeper breaths and invite yourself to be fully present for this ritual. Light a candle as you speak your intention to cultivate a deeper connection with your well and benevolent ancient ancestors. Welcome your team of guides and helpers, asking them to surround you with their protection and love and help create a strong and safe container for this ritual.

Feeding the dead – Let your ancestors know you are here to spend time with them, welcoming them with songs and offerings to create a feast for them to enjoy. Smudge some rosemary or mugwort to help activate the pathways of remembrance within you. When the altar feels alive and humming, start drumming, rattling or rhythm-ically tapping or clapping – you can also use a drumming track (see Resources, page 190). Maintain this rhythm until you notice a subtle shift in your perception.

Circle of stones – Choose stones from your altar and, one-by-one, place them in a circle around you. Feel the sense of support and containment this brings. Imagine that each stone represents a wise, loving, ancient ancestor who you can relate with and receive guidance from. In this space you can engage with them directly by holding a stone and asking them a question, or beginning a conversation however you feel moved to. You may like to work with just one stone and return to do this ritual again, creating deeper connections with each of them. Or you can go around the circle, receiving different perspectives from this council of elders.

Remembering to remember – When you feel the conversation naturally comes to a close, hold your bowl of water close to your heart and speak aloud your gratitude for your ancestors. Add a generous pinch of salt to the water and watch it dissolve, as a gesture of carrying forward the stories of your kin. Dip a sprig of rosemary into the salty water and sprinkle over the stones and your ancestral altar as you sing or hum in praise. Using sacred herbs, thoroughly cleanse yourself from head to toe with the aromatic smoke, demanding for all energy that is not yours to leave. Thank all your helpers and guides for their protection as you blow out the candle to complete this part of the ritual.

Tree temple – Carry your bowl of water, either in the bowl or transfer it to a bottle, to a tree nearby that provides another connection place for you and your ancestors. Pour the salty water over the roots of the tree, offering your blessings to all ancestors, human and more-than-human, and to the deep, winding roots of memory that lie within the earth. Lay down any extra offerings of food or seeds, creating a place you can return to make offerings to the spirit of your ancestors. Sing a song as a closing of this space.

Holding council – You can repeat the circle of stones part of this ritual as often as you choose, as a way of deepening your relationship with your ancestors. Keep your eight stones in a pouch or box that you can adorn with symbols from your interactions with your council of elders.

Winter

The Dance of Winter

Once the birds and squirrels have gathered their supply of nuts and seeds for the winter and the trees have shed their leaves, there is a quiet in the natural world that is marked by its stillness. When the Earth is blanketed in snow it truly feels as though the whole world is asleep, tucked up for a long night of collective dreaming. And yet I spot a wren dancing in the hedgerow, the flash of a kingfisher as it darts downstream, fox pawprints, and the proud parents of two cygnets circling the lake, their bright feathers elevating them to regal standing among the snowy surroundings.

Winter provides brief joys that are so arresting and thrilling because they are fleeting and are not guaranteed. A frosty dawn when everything is glistening, the sudden swell of starlings as they perform their swirling sky-dance, meeting the eyes of a deer through the bare branches – all feel like miracles to witness. When I feel a proximity to death, deep in the bones of winter, the sacred comes into focus with a startling clarity that arises from knowing the closeness between life and death and the impermanence of things.

Although most of the garden sleeps through winter as plants draw their energy downwards, going dormant above ground, 'dying back', there are some hardy blooms that still flower. My heart always leaps when I spot a winter-flowering cherry tree or the first snowdrop. These flowers sing of the promise of spring while the rest of the soil is covered in mulch, protecting the seeds hidden in the darkness of the dreaming earth.

Then there are my beloved trees – bare, outstretched, surrendering themselves to the lick of winter. In their skeletal form they reveal the twists and turns of their journey through life, their beautiful networks of branches and hidden nests, and they are perfect for climbing. I could lie for hours on a beech branch watching for signs of movement in the tranquil winter woodland. When my son and I go exploring in January, we like to play 'spot the elf cap', looking out for the scarlet fungus that pops with unexpected colour. If we're very quiet, we might spot the bright zing of lime-yellow wings that belong to the brimstone butterfly, fluttering near ivy or holly where they hibernate. Even in the coldest months, there is life that thrives.

The essence of winter

Walking somewhere wild on a winter's night, with the cool air awakening my senses and a sea of bright, shimmering stars sweeping above, is one of my greatest joys. Breathing deeply until my nostrils tickle from the cold, I feel a sense of belonging with the winter. As the longer nights draw in, I feel a cloak surrounding me, inviting me to turn inwards and retreat into my winter cave, to rest and regenerate in the quiet stillness as I surrender to the darkness. I feel at home here. There is a quality of sanctuary and rootedness that comes from the connection with the Earth Element in this portal of winter.

As your energy is drawn inwards and downwards there is an unravelling from the outer world, enabling you to integrate all that has been learnt from the past cycle of growth. Although it appears that the natural world is dormant beneath our feet, as within us in the darkness, miracles are unfolding. Within the seeds there is a stirring, an emergence of life that takes places in the dark, when unseen creative forces are at play. From the fertile nothingness, the first sparks of life emerge.

Being willing to enter into the darkness is a strength often overlooked in modern cultures. Through welcoming the winter and intentionally crossing the threshold into darkness, you can transform

your relationship with your fear and with death. By releasing control and surrendering to the great mystery, you touch upon death and learn how to die. From learning how to die well, you learn how to live more fully. Through your willingness to meet the darkness, you are initiated into a life of fullness wherein everything is recognised as sacred. Death and grief are seen as the catalysts for opening your heart to more beauty and wonder so that you experience your wholeness, your holiness, and the cyclical wisdom of life, death and rebirth.

Winter's wisdom is embodied in the archetype of the crone, hag, the Cailleach or Beira in Scottish folklore. She is intuitive, insightful, direct and confident, a weaver of stories that enrich the imagination and speak of home. As an elder who has walked the old roads, she is able to hold space for the transformation of others, a midwife to our rebirth. Associated with the phase of the dark moon, the winter portal invites you to attend to the liminal space in between realms, to hone your psychic abilities by withdrawing from the outer world and entering the cave of unknowing, to embrace your solitude and prepare for the initiation of death and rebirth that comes each winter. In this crucible of transformation, you are listening to a deeper current, guided by an innate knowing, incubating your dreams and visions for the future.

Ways to attune to the energy of winter

Listening to the instinct to retreat inwards and hibernate during winter is vital if you are going to allow this powerful portal to work on you. You need to say 'yes' to the darkness and welcome the opportunity to meet yourself in your fullness, bare like the trees, with nowhere to hide. Entering this season intentionally will enable you to drink more deeply from the well of wisdom winter has to offer. Opening your ears to listen to the silence and surrendering to the fertile darkness will ensure you emerge in spring renewed and inspired, ready for rebirth.

In the cave of winter, you can attune to the energies more deeply by spending time in darkness, aligning with your natural circadian rhythms by resting when it is dark and avoiding the use of screens and artificial light. Candles, firelight or Himalayan salt lamps will create a more natural lighting that invites your body to soften and enter this time of dreaming. As you slow down in the darker months, you can become more present to the Earth of you, your physical body, and the subtle signals she gives you throughout the day. Listening to what she needs and enjoys as you create a sanctuary to unravel and delve into the darkness.

Most crafts or hobbies that use your hands will support a slowing down and help calm your nervous system. Winter is the time to knit, stitch, whittle and mend. As you make, you are connecting with the winter energies of transformation, creating and reforming something. Fill up with inspiration by visioning and dreaming, using your imaginative faculties to create an image of the world you wish to see. You can journal or undertake shamanic-style journeys to access your soul's deeper longing. Enrich your imagination by listening to stories by candlelight or reading books on rainy days. It's also important to create space in your life for not-doing, embracing the quietude and respite that winter brings so your energy can be directed within, to regenerate and transform.

During the cold months of winter, there is a harshness in the natural world that can be reflected within your mind. There were times that I dreaded winter and the darkness that crept in as I found myself spiralling into depression, stifled by negativity, overwhelmed and seeing the world through a self-orientated and dark grey lens. The darkness felt suffocating. So I learnt ways to stoke my inner fire through spiritual practice, kindling the courage I needed to welcome the darkness and the potential for transformation. I found ways to shift my mood with dance, prayer, breathwork, drumming and singing, and by opening my heart to others in recognition of the darkness and death we all must face in our lives. Through simple acts of kindness to your human and more-than-human kin, you can expand your conscious web of connection and feelings of intimacy and togetherness, shaking off the lonely winter blues. I find that the more kindness I show to others, the more I direct towards myself and see in the world around me.

Daily rituals

Food blessing

For at least one meal a day, create a personalised ritual to bless your food. You could light a candle and take some deep breaths that fill your heart space, before blowing this loving energy on to your food. Or hold your hands above your plate, imagining golden light from the palms of your hands beaming on to your food, like the Sun that made them. You can include other family members, singing a song with your children before you start to eat, or speaking aloud a blessing together such as:

'Earth who gives to us our food
Sun who makes it ripe and good
Dearest Earth and dearest Sun
Joy and love for all you've done'

Body appreciation

When you're getting ready for bed, before dressing in your pyjamas, spend a few minutes thanking your body, being intimate with her, touching or massaging yourself in ways that feel responsive to your body's needs. Be sure to thank your feet for everywhere they have taken you today and how they keep you grounded. Move up and around your body, expressing what you appreciate about your various body parts, including your organs within. Bring kind attention to those parts you don't like, that are problematic or have experienced trauma. Finish with one hand on your heart and the other on your belly, as you whisper aloud, 'thank you, I love you, I honour you'.

Small acts of kindness

Choose a small act of kindness each day that will enrich the life of another. It could be litter-picking, a little note of loveliness left for a stranger on a park bench, a book left on the seat of the bus, feeding the birds, calling a friend to tell them how much you appreciate them, writing a letter to a relative, letting someone go in front of you in a queue or offering to pay someone's shortfall at the checkout. Imagine this gesture of kindness rippling out from your heart, meeting another's and creating more ripples of kindness throughout the world.

Tree time

If you are able to visit a tree outdoors this is a beautiful daily ritual, but I also encourage you to try this using your imagination when you are inside. Focus on your connection with the earth through your feet, take some deeper breaths as you expand your awareness and approach a tree. You might like to introduce yourself as you circle clockwise round the tree, sensing the merging of your energy fields. When you feel drawn to sit or stand with your back against the tree, drop deeper into your body awareness to feel the sensations and what arises for you when contacting the tree and you feel the support and strength the tree offers you. When you feel filled up, say thank you to the tree and give it a hug.

Worry stone

Keep a small stone beside your bed for sharing your worries with before you go to sleep. Holding the stone in your hand, speak aloud your concerns or worries, anything you struggled with or regret about your day that you wish to let go of. Speak with kindness to yourself, as though talking to a child. When you conclude your words, blow a long out-breath onto the stone, thank it for carrying away and transmuting your worries, giving it a kiss if you like. Place the stone under your pillow or hold it in your hand as you go to sleep, enabling this alchemy to occur.

Key Qualities of Winter's Energy

ASSOCIATIONS

Night, Earth, north, dark moon, death and rebirth, crone archetype, ancestors, elders, initiation, belonging, physical healing, dreaming, composting, darkness, spinning, weaving, solitude, the hermit, storytelling, silence, cave, the void, transformation, roots, touch, menstruation

CHARACTERISTICS

Rest, recovery, hibernation, perseverance, tenacity, incubation, gestation, stillness, listening, tranquillity, contemplation, surrender, integration, consolidation, regeneration, nurturing, grounding, renewal

COLOURS

Greens, blues, browns, white, red, black

FLOWERS AND PLANTS

Yew, oak, holly, ivy, blackthorn, alder, pine, cedar, mistletoe, moss, lichen

SYMBOLS

Rocks, stones, bones, seeds, caves, crystals, branches of evergreens, star-shaped seed pods, stars, red berries, fly agaric mushrooms, milk, gifts, wreaths, Yule log, drum

ANIMALS

Stag, raven, wolf, bear, badger, mole, cow, earthworm

The Golden Shield
A ritual for invoking protection
and support for challenging times

When you are facing a time of uncertainty, a crisis of mind, body or spirit, or are just having one of those days when nothing seems to be going your way and you feel out of kilter, it can be extremely helpful to craft a ritual that reminds you of the support available to you from the more-than-human world.

With the pervading worldview perpetuating our separation and that only what we can *see* is real, we miss so much of the potential that is available for us to tap into from the greater Web of Life. By calling upon these invisible allies for protection and guidance you can cultivate a deep sense of belonging and trust that knows that no matter what happens, life has your back.

This ritual is designed to connect you to your inner power source so that you can access the wealth of invisible support available to you and create a shield of protection around you. Once you have carried out this ritual, you will have the tools to produce your golden shield at any moment, when you want to preserve your energy or to ensure you feel strengthened when going into a challenging situation.

INGREDIENTS

Smudge stick or
herbs and charcoal disc

Cushion

Bowl of water

Towel

Objects and totems
of power

Shawl or blanket

Candle and lighter

Piece of card

Colouring pens/pencils

Preparation – Consider what items you would like to include in your circle of protection. These might be natural subjects, such as shells, stones and branches, sacred items in your home, and those that carry significant memories, empower you or remind you of loved ones that you wish to include in your circle. Gather them together.

Create the space – Start by cleansing your ritual space energetically with sound or smudging herbs, and physically, leaving an area on the ground to create a circle roughly 1–1.5 metres (3–5ft) in diameter. Have ready in the centre your cushion, shawl and paper and pens. Light a candle as you speak your intention to the flame, asking to gather together all your support and power, seen and unseen, to help create a circle of protection and golden shield. Take three deep belly breaths as you allow your words to sink in.

Clear your energetic field – Wash your hands and face in the water, dry them, shake your body and jump up and down, encouraging all unwanted energy to be released from your feet into the earth.

Welcoming your allies – Standing upright, breathe deeply and close your eyes. Feel your feet on the earth and the depth of strength beneath. Acknowledge how you are always held up and supported no matter what. Kneel and place one item that represents Earth in the area surrounding your cushion to create the beginning of your circle.

Stay kneeling outside the circle as you ask for all your guides and those allies who support you to gather round and show them-selves. Open your heart, relax your mind and invite your intuitive and imaginal faculties to the fore. Whether it is your great-grand-father, the goddess Artemis or your national rugby team – welcome all those who arise in your consciousness, thanking them for their support as you give them a place in your circle by putting down a subject to represent them. If you don't have a clear sense of individuals or names, feel if you can sense any presence, welcoming them just the same, until you have created a circle with your allies.

Feeling the embrace – When your circle is complete, imagine the space within the circle filling with vibrant golden light, creating a cylinder of energy that goes way up through the sky and beyond. Shake your body, loosen up, and take three intentional breaths as you prepare to enter this sacred circle from an embodied stance. Step across the threshold into the circle, feeling the golden light filling your cells and the loving embrace of all those surrounding you.

Visioning your shield – Sit down on the cushion and wrap the shawl around you, imagining one of your allies placing this protective shawl upon your shoulders. Close your eyes and quieten your mind, as you allow the golden light to infuse you more deeply. Imagine this cylinder of light around you, allowing only kind and loving energy into your space. Feel what it is like in your body to know this level of support and containment. To feel safe and unconditionally loved.

Bring your attention to your third eye on your brow, call upon your guides for assistance as you ask for the symbol of your shield to be revealed in a way you can interpret. Do not overthink this, just let what wants to come, come. If you struggle with this, draw a circle on the paper, stare at it, and see if a symbol emerges there.

Design your shield – When you have a sense of the symbol, open your eyes, draw a circle on the piece of paper and draw your shield symbol within it. Gaze at it awhile, then practise drawing the symbol in the air in front of you. This symbol activates your golden shield, which you can imagine in your third eye or draw in the air whenever you want to engage the cellular memory of this circle of protection.

Everyday use – Each day take a few minutes to intentionally enter the circle of protection, call in your spirit helpers and all that supports you. Do this in your mind's eye, or make a physical circle with scarves for you to enter. You can practise recreating this feeling throughout your day, sensing the golden cylinder that surrounds and protects you whenever you draw your shield symbol in the air.

In the End is the Beginning
Circular pilgrimage to let go of old ways and choose a new direction

When you experience transitions in your life it might take some time to adjust to and accept the changes, especially if they were not expected. There can often be beliefs or burdens that make it difficult to embrace a new beginning unfettered. I have found walking a pilgrimage one of the most simple and effective rituals for helping me make peace with what is unfolding in my life, to remember that the journey is shaping me in unexpected and beautiful ways, and all I have to do is put one foot in front of the other. Simply walking in relationship with the natural world is also incredibly grounding when you feel off-centre; it invites you to come home to yourself and the Earth.

A pilgrimage is a journey made on foot to a sacred place, initiated with an intention. It provides a ritual space for you to attend to what is present and emerging in your life. Perhaps you need to adjust to a transition or are seeking a new direction. You might dedicate your journey to something you want clarity on or to give thanks in some way. A pilgrimage usually involves laying down a burden or releasing something so that you return lighter and clearer about the path ahead.

Setting your intention elevates a walk to a sacred quest, as moving through a landscape reflects the inner journey and creates the container for healing and insight to come forth. Pay attention to synchronicities, omens or symbols you see within the natural world, for they all carry significance on a pilgrimage.

INGREDIENTS

Walking boots

Stone

Offerings/
birdseed

Windproof lighter

Journal and pen

Plastic bag

Note – With this ritual I suggest walking a circular route because returning to the beginning at the end imbues the journey with a particular flavour that reflects the cyclical dance we make through life. It can also be immensely rewarding to repeat your pilgrimage route at different times of year to appreciate the natural life cycles inherent in the seasons and how these affect you.

Preparation – Consider where you would like to walk your pilgrimage. I love to study maps and look for historical and sacred sites, springs and waterways or go online to research the whereabouts of ancient trees so I can create a pilgrimage around a place of significant interest to me. There may be sites connected with your ancestors that are calling for you to visit.

Keep your intention in mind while you are planning. Listen in to whether certain landscapes or Elements feel more aligned. Including water is helpful if you want support with letting go of something. Climbing hills and walking cliffs with far-reaching views will expand your perspective if you are looking for clarity or a new direction in life.

Setting your intention – Before you begin, hold your stone in your hand and connect with your intention by breathing deeply into your belly, imagining roots from your feet piercing the soil beneath. Clarify your motivation for walking this pilgrimage and write down your intention. Keep this on a piece of paper in your pocket, alongside some offerings for the places you will be attending. Call in your guides and spirit allies to be with you as you make this journey. Through walking this pilgrimage, ask that you remember the depth of your relationship with the Earth, dissolving any sense of separation with the natural world.

Walking with love – As you start walking, carrying your stone in your hand, invite your mind to settle and your attention to inhabit your body and the landscape, allowing the boundaries to gradually dissolve. Pay attention to your breath and the rhythm of your feet on the earth. Imagine with each step you are kissing the earth. Drink in the beauty of the landscape and amplify your sense of wonder and appreciation at the views and sites along the way.

Releasing your burden – Notice what thoughts or memories arise as you walk on your journey. Are there repeating thoughts, worries or feelings? When you bring your intention to mind, are there obstacles or limiting beliefs that make it difficult for you to accept change, or are there people or ideas that you need to let go of to move forward? Imagine the stone in your hand drawing out all these thoughts. There will be a point on your journey when it feels right to release the burdens you carry – perhaps a river, on top of a hill, or within the roots of a tree. Speak anything aloud to the stone that you want to let go of, before throwing, burying or washing them away with a moment of ceremony to acknowledge this emancipation. Leave some offerings for the spirits of the place in gratitude for their witnessing and healing.

Praising places – As you continue on your pilgrimage, make space for giving thanks, expressing your appreciation for the natural world by leaving offerings of birdseed at places you rest, feel touched by or experience a moment of insight. You might like to sing your praises too, or recite a poem. Practise seeing with an open heart and offering blessings to the various kin you meet along the way. Keep an eye out for litter, pick it up and keep it in a plastic bag to dispose of after your journey.

Embracing change – As you conclude your pilgrimage, find somewhere to sit awhile. Reflect on your intention as you write in your journal and record any significant insights or reflections. Are there any commitments to make to support you moving forward in your life and embracing change? Speak these aloud. To close the ritual container, ignite the paper that has your intention on, setting it to the ground or letting it be carried by the wind.

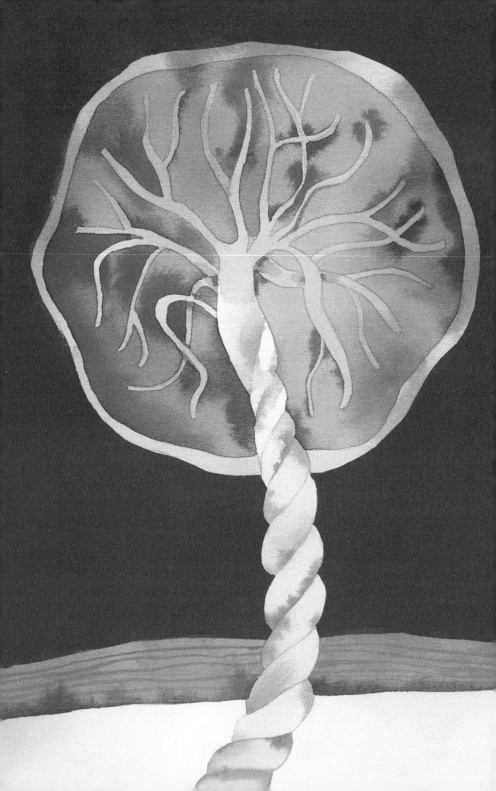

Coming Home to Earth
A ritual to cultivate belonging and awaken your purpose

When I was pregnant with my son, I took part in a workshop that explored the shamanic dimensions of pregnancy, an eye-opening journey that revealed how cut off I had been from my instinctive knowing of how to birth life, and how lost we are as a culture in terms of honouring our significant rites of passage and valuing Earth-based wisdom.

I was introduced to a ritual from a book by Aboriginal elder Minmia, *Under the Quandong Tree*, that spoke to this place of longing in me and is the inspiration for this ritual. It is based on the wisdom that everyone has a unique blueprint, a 'Miwi', that holds the coded instructions for our life's journey; it is akin to a spiritual map that is activated through its union with the earth. The blueprint is found in the placenta we are born connected with, and so traditionally the placenta is buried in the earth as part of a birthing ceremony, allowing this unique map to be grounded so that the individual can be guided through life, aligned with their true purpose, with a marrow-deep knowing that they are connected with Gaia.

I was mesmerised when I saw my son's placenta, adorned with vessels branching out from the twisted column of the umbilical cord, closely resembling an actual tree with its branches and roots. I later buried it as part of a ritual with my family, a tradition honoured across cultures, but I also wanted to recreate this birthing ceremony for myself even though I had no placenta. With the following ritual I was able to do so, choosing to visit a yew tree in the Forest of Dean, where I wanted to come home to Gaia, my primordial mother, and activate my unique codes to guide me on my way. Ideally you should carry out this ritual near to where you were born, but if this is not possible then choose somewhere that you feel a soul connection with.

INGREDIENTS

Stone to represent
your placenta

Small bowl of water

Flowers

Trowel

Scissors

Candle, jar and lighter

Journal and pen

Smudge stick or
herbs and charcoal disc

Three twigs

Preparation – When you feel called to perform this ritual, ask Gaia to give you a stone that represents your placenta. Be attentive to how this might come to you, perhaps on a walk or gifted to you by someone. Trust it will arrive at the perfect moment and you will know they are the one fit for this purpose.

Choose a time to perform this ritual that is spacious, perhaps making a day of it and creating a pilgrimage around arriving at the place you wish to rebirth yourself. As part of the journey you can gather your three twigs, choosing those suspended in branches that have not yet touched the ground.

Meeting the earth – When you arrive at your chosen place, lay down your things, keeping your sticks off the ground by placing them on something. Take off your shoes and meet the earth with your feet, feeling the contact and intimacy nourishing you all the way through your body. Kneeling down, place your offering of flowers on the earth. With your hands on the soil, introduce yourself and speak your intention for being here. Ask the spirit of the place for permission to carry out this ritual and listen for a clear 'yes' before continuing.

Purifying with smoke – Light your candle and place it in a jar as you welcome your spirit helpers, guides, and benevolent ancestors to witness your rebirthing. Feel their love and support surrounding you. Using the sacred smoke from igniting your herbs or smudge stick, cleanse your body from head to toe, allowing all negative energy to evaporate and transmute into the light of love as you take some deeper breaths into your belly.

Return to the womb – Using your trowel, dig a small hole in the earth, singing or humming as you work. Place your placenta stone in the bowl of water, acknowledging how your placenta was carried in the waters of your mother's womb, giving you life force to grow. Take your time with this, allow any memories to surface.

Rebirthing – Remove your placenta stone from the water and lay it on your lap. Cut some strands of your hair and place on top of the stone or wrap around it if long enough. Spit some saliva on top to bind the hair to the stone, sealing this unique energetic blueprint together. Speak some words of praise for life and your longing to belong before placing the stone into the hole with the hair facing downwards. Lie down with your belly on the earth, mouth over the hole, and take 40 deep, intentional breaths, staying present to the sensations in your body.

Commitments – Gently return to kneeling beside the hole. With the twigs you have gathered, listen deeply to your heart-wisdom and speak aloud a commitment with each one – one for yourself, one for your family and community and one for Gaia. After speaking each commitment, bend the twig until it snaps and place it in the hole on top of your placenta stone. As you refill the hole with soil, ask the Earth to accept the symbolic placenta and for your unique codes to be activated. Ask for the courage, compassion and wisdom you need to embody this truth on earth. Give thanks for her holding and power. Offer a blessing to this place of your rebirth – read a poem or scatter some wildflower seeds or birdseed. Jump three times on the place of the hole to finish and state aloud, 'And so it is' before you blow out the candle to close the ritual space.

Spend some time in reflection at this spot, allowing the experience to integrate. Write down your commitments in your journal so you can revisit them. Go gently with yourself the remainder of the day, enjoying more time outdoors and a wild swim or water dip to enhance this experience of rebirth.

Dance of the Dark
Befriending your shadow-self and transforming fear

One of the legacies of patriarchy and its religious systems is the prevailing fear of the darkness, causing us to strive for the light in an attempt to transcend our earthly bodies and repress the wild and fertile potential of the unknown. The dance of light and dark features in so many myths and religious ideologies, playing out as a battle where light must overcome dark, the forces of good overcoming the power of evil, the masculine dominating the feminine.

Many of these myths are rooted in binary beliefs that perpetuate separation, dishonouring the fullness of the human experience and psyche. The yin-yang symbol demonstrates beautifully how light and dark can exist in harmony and balance, flowing symbiotically between one another, also carrying the seed of the other within them. They are not separate but diverse parts of the whole.

And so it is within us humans. From my work with clients it is painfully evident how imbalanced we have become, with most experiencing a lack of purpose, true sense of self or appreciation of their gifts. We have become dismembered by modern culture and the systems we live in, striving for an ideal that cuts us off from our roots and our soul's longing by valuing what is rational and visible and denying the potential and power within the unseen, imaginal and darkness.

Your shadow-self includes both repressed, instinctual feelings and untapped potential – that which you have left behind or forgotten in an attempt to conform and gain approval. By integrating those wholesome parts of your shadow and welcoming the creative potential and mystery that is within the darkness, you can loosen the grip of fear and explore your shadow-self with curiosity and acceptance.

Creating a mask in a ritual context is a powerful way to delve into your persona and give expression to hidden parts of yourself that are not approved of – negative characteristics such as envy, greed and hatred – and also other aspects such as creativity, self-confidence and healthy anger. By facing what you fear, you are able to transform your relationship with and understanding of the power of darkness.

INGREDIENTS

Smudge stick or
herbs and charcoal
disc

Journal

Blindfold

Blanket

Candle and lighter

Biodegradable white
mask (available from
craft shops or online)

Paints and paintbrush

Music

An apple

Preparation – Set aside time to journal around the theme of your shadow-self. What is your relationship with it? How do you relate to darkness? What parts of yourself are you ashamed of? What aspects have you hidden to conform to others' expectations? Explore the fears you carry about what dwells in your shadow-self.

Prepare the space – Cleanse your ritual space thoroughly with herbal smoke and create a safe container by welcoming the directions and Elements. Light a candle that you are dedicating to this shadow-work, stating your intention aloud as you gaze into the flame. Ask your guides and spirit helpers to hold a strong and protective circle around you for the duration of this ritual.

Shadow journey – Lie down with your blanket around you and place your blindfold over your eyes. Take some deep breaths, sighing on the out-breath as you bring your awareness inwards and settle your mind. Using your imagination, see yourself entering a house, crossing the threshold into a corridor where you see stairs going downwards. Go down the stairs into the dimly lit basement where you see a row of doors. On the other side of these doors are aspects of your shadow-self. Choose one door, walk towards it and open it.

Whatever follows in this space relates to an aspect of your shadow-self. Ask their name and any questions you have as you are taken on an imaginary journey. Allow this part of yourself space to be revealed, to share and express themselves without judgement. Notice what feelings arise and any symbols that draw your attention.

Returning – When you feel you have met this aspect of your shadow-self fully, thank them for their gifts and wisdom. Return to the door in the basement, go through it and close it behind you. Climb the stairs and leave the house out of the main door, closing it behind you.

Mask-making – Slowly open your eyes, coming back to your body and the physical environment that surrounds you. Pick up your mask and paintbrush as you recall your journey with your shadow-self. What did you feel? Were there any symbols you saw? What words came up? Is there a name you could give to this part of yourself?

Start painting on to the mask, inviting your hands to move freely as you let go of any judgement of the outcome. Allow feelings to come to the surface, and release energy through sound if that helps them be expressed.

Dancing with your darkness – When you feel a sense of completion, sit and gaze at your mask, aware of any responses you experience internally. You might like to journal about your experience and what you learnt about this aspect of your shadow-self. Let the paint dry enough so you can handle it, turn on a playlist that speaks to your wilder side and secure the mask on to your face, as you invite this aspect of your shadow-self to be expressed through you. Use your body as an instrument to play the tune of this persona, giving them space to dance/rage/wail/shout/beg in an embodied way. Go on a journey with this aspect of yourself, staying open and curious, until the energy settles and you feel a natural conclusion to your movement.

Integration – Remove the mask and look at it. Share your gratitude for this part of you and make the commitment to stay attentive to your shadow-self, discerning what gifts are there to reclaim and what needs to remain hidden, although seen and integrated. Blow out your candle to close the ritual space as you offer your thanks to all those who were present.

Eat an apple to assimilate and digest your experience, burying the core in your garden or the soil of a houseplant as a blessing to the dark, fertile earth where the shadow dwells. Journal your reflections.

You can repeat this ritual, opening different doors in the basement of the house, to explore more parts of your shadow-self. Create a series of masks that you can adorn, dialogue and dance with when you feel your shadow-self activated, to get greater clarity on what their triggers are and what they want to express. When you feel an aspect of your shadow-self has been well integrated, you may choose to ritually burn or bury that mask in recognition of your healing journey.

Honouring Death,
Celebrating Life
A ritual to honour the death of
a loved one and cultivate remembrance

Funerary rites in the modern, Western world are often diminished to static and sombre affairs that stifle the wild expression of grief and potential for deepening our appreciation and understanding of death. The need to create a container for grief to be witnessed and an authentic ritual that honours the life and personality of the departed is slowly becoming better understood as a vital process for coming to terms with the loss of a loved one.

This ritual provides a framework for creating a more meaningful funeral and can also be crafted for a memorial on the anniversary of the date your loved one passed away, or to create a burial ritual for a beloved pet who has died. I hope it will provide inspiration for you to consider other creative ways to commemorate death that reflect the life being honoured, and the constellation of those present at a funerary rite. In an intimate family setting with children, for instance, there might be playful ways to help them understand the realm of grief and death and the cycles of life. I offer a suggestion for including children below, but it can be a deeply connective experience to explore ritual ideas with others who are grieving and with children themselves.

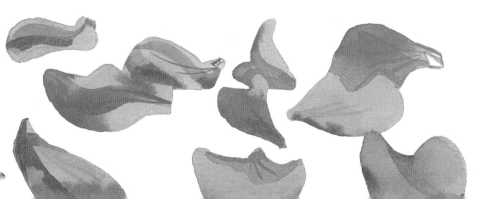

INGREDIENTS

Altar cloth
and adornments

Bowl of water

Salt

Rose petals

Candles
and lighter

A reading/poem

Songs

Bubbles

Envelopes
of wildflower
seeds

*Guests bring a stone and a photo
or an object to add to the story altar
that honours the departed.*

Preparation – You will need to consider the location for this ritual, preferably outside, where you can gather in relative privacy. It may be somewhere you can revisit and tend to as a place of remembrance in a garden or a significant place for the departed.

Send out invites to those you wish to attend, asking them to bring a stone and a photo or object that relates to the person who has died.

Ahead of the ritual, choose a poem or reading and some songs that speak to the life of the departed. Set up an altar space that you can gather around in a circle; laying down a cloth on a table or tray, with two bowls – one with water, the other salt – candles and flowers, and any other items that elevate the sanctity of the space.

Coming together – Once people have arrived, come together in a circle and take three intentional breaths to help everyone arrive fully in the space before you share the intention for this gathering, to celebrate the life and honour the death of the departed. Welcome the directions and Elements and any other energies you wish to be present, inviting others to welcome their guides and helpers too – either inwardly with a few moments' silence, or spontaneously naming them aloud once the space has been created to do so. Join together in making a collective sound, followed by a song or poem, and a few minutes of silence for people to connect with their grief in their own way.

Story altar – Invite the guests to take it in turn to share about the item they have brought for the story altar and what it represents. You can also offer prompts such as 'what was your relationship with the departed?', 'In what ways did they touch your life?' and 'what are the lasting memories you have from your time with them?'. Once they have offered their story, invite them to place their item on the story altar in the centre and add a pinch of salt to the bowl of water, after letting everyone know that each grain of salt represents an aspect of the life being acknowledged. As the salt becomes a part of the water, it holds the memories and carries forward their stories. Once complete, spend some time together in silence, allowing everyone to drink in the memories of the person they are grieving.

Cairn of mourning – With everyone holding their stone in their hand, open up the space for people to express their grief, however that comes naturally for them, placing their stone on the earth near the altar when they have finished speaking. The stones can be arranged in an organic formation, balancing them on top of one another, placing them in a circle, or next to one another.

When everyone has laid their stone and shared their grief, pour the bowl of salty water over the stones and join together in singing a song or making a collective sound. The stones can remain there to create a place of memorial for people to visit, or if inside they can be taken to a river or the ocean and offered up to the collective waters.

Blessing the journey ahead – One by one, move around the circle as everyone speaks a short blessing, sharing their gratitude and appreciation for the person who has died. After everyone has spoken, distribute a bowl of rose petals and invite the guests to scatter petals around the cairn and story altar as a way of creating a path for the deceased to journey on, or if appropriate they can blow bubbles, sending their blessings with the spirit of the dead up to the skies, and to mark the completion of this ritual.

Seeds of remembrance – Give everyone a small envelope filled with wildflower seeds to take away and ask them to scatter them somewhere special. Invite them to take a moment as they plant or scatter the seeds to share a prayer or words of remembrance for the departed.

Variations

With children, you can include crafting memory boats for this ritual, using a piece of tree bark decorated with objects from the natural environment, such as petals, moss and feathers. At the story altar, invite them to write or draw messages of love to the departed. When you have access to a body of water, place the messages on the bark and set the boat adrift on a stream or river. This can offer a gentle way to release and grieve and follows on well from burying a beloved pet.

This ritual can be adapted to honour the loss of a miscarriage when crafted as a couple, creating a memory box in place of the story altar, adding objects that represent this life lost and your grief. You can either bury this box or keep it somewhere you can revisit and attend to your grief. Choose somewhere to hold this ritual that you can both return to and connect with as a place to grieve, remember and heal your hearts. You may like to plant a flower or tree to honour the memory of the life lost.

If you wish to create a solitary space for remembering, you can simplify this ritual, scaling it back to the ritual elements. Use the space to offer a stone to the earth as an opportunity to say anything you felt was unsaid or you wish to express to the person who has died, and conclude by offering a blessing to the departed by scattering petals or creating a mandala of flowers.

Afterword

'You are not a drop in the ocean. You are the entire ocean in a drop.'
– Rumi

When this book began forming, I commenced a daily ritual of gathering water from the nearby River Brue, and carrying them in loving prayer to the horse chestnut tree in my garden. I poured the water onto the roots and surrounding earth where I had buried my intention bundle for this book, to fertilise those dream-seeds and feed the spirits of this place that I live with. It became a way of courting these spirits, relating with them more intimately and intentionally, enriching my sense of purpose and responsibility to care for those who uphold and inspire me.

Each morning as I walked with the waters, I felt the preciousness of carrying this life in my hands, infused with all the prayers, tears and tides of those who came before. One autumnal day, as I poured the water onto the soil, I tuned into the rhythm of the waters in my blood and imagined the waters within and without weaving a new pathway together, replenishing and restoring to life all that is sacred, all that is love. I felt the seeds of hope awaken to this potential, of how we can change the world by changing the stories we weave. When we collaborate with the forces and elements of nature and the more-than-human world, we harmonise with nature's principles, expand our sense of what's possible and receive inspiration that can help us reimagine our collective narrative.

The ritual life is a way of remembering, relating, and storytelling; inviting you to be a conscious participant in creating the world you long for. Through nurturing the Four Seeds of intention, creativity, gratitude and kindness, and planting them in your life, you can cultivate a meaningful existence, aligned with your values, and build pathways of reciprocity and regeneration. As you take responsibility for your life and the reality you're constructing, you grow yourself up, becoming an initiated human being – no longer a helpless child dependent on Mother Earth but a passionate lover and caretaker of the world. Instead of asking 'what do I need?', the question becomes 'what can I give?', as you become human in the fullest possible way, preparing to ripen as a true elder.

Now is the time to dare to love greatly, dream wildly, share innovative stories, craft soulful rituals and midwife the birth of this new world, born from your deepest longing, and the innate knowing that *you are nature –* a seed carrier of the beautiful future to come.

Resources

I am including here a selection of books that have inspired me on my journey or informed the writing of this book, and an array of other resources to support the blossoming of your ritual life.

Books

Abram, David. *The Spell of the Sensuous*. Vintage Books, 1997.

Ayot, William. *Re-enchanting the Forest*. Sleeping Mountain Press, 2016.

Beck, Renee, and Metrick, Sydney Barbara. *The Art of Ritual: Creating and Performing Ceremonies for Growth and Change*. Apocryphile Press, 2018.

Blackie, Sharon. *If Women Rose Rooted, A Life-changing Journey to Authenticity and Belonging*. September Publishing, 2019.

Bridges, William. *Making Sense of Life's Transitions, Strategies for Coping with the Difficult, Painful, and Confusing Times in Your Life*. Addison-Wesley Publishing Company, 1980.

Capra, Fritjof. *The Web of Life: A New Scientific Understanding of Living Systems*. Anchor Books, 1996.

Curran, Dr. Bob. *Celtic Lore & Legend*. Career Press, 2004.

Edinger, Edward F. *Ego & Archetype*. Shambala Publications Inc., 1992.

Farmer, Steven D. *Sacred Ceremony, How to Create Ceremonies for Healing, Transitions, and Celebrations*. Hay House, 2002.

Foor, Daniel. *Ancestral Medicine, Rituals for Personal and Family Healing*. Bear & Company, 2017.

Forest, Danu. *Celtic Tree Magic, Ogham Lore and Druid Mysteries*. Llewellyn Publications, 2014.

Ingerman, Sandra. *The Book of Ceremony*, Sounds True, 2018.

Jacobs, Joseph (editor). *Celtic Fairy Tales*. Senate, 1994.

Jung, C.G. *The Archetypes and the Collective Unconscious (Collected Works of C. G. Jung)*. Routledge, 1999.

Kimmerer, Robin Wall. *Braiding Sweetgrass. Indigenous Wisdom, Scientific Knowledge and the Teachings of Plants*. Milkweed Editions, 2013.

Kindred, Glennie. *Creating Ceremony*. Glennie Kindred, 2002.

Kindred, Glennie. *Earth Alchemy: A Dynamic Fusion Between Alchemy and the Eight Celtic Festivals*. Hay House UK, 2013.

Kindred, Glennie. *Earth Wisdom: A Heartwarming Mixture of the Spiritual, the Practical and the Proactive*. Hay House UK, 2011.

Kindred, Glennie. *Sacred Earth Celebrations*. Permanent Publication, 2014.

Kindred, Glennie. *Walking with Trees*. Permanent Publications, 2019.

Lee, Scout Cloud (editor). *The Circle is Sacred, A Medicine Book for Women*. Council Oak Books, 1995.

Linn, Denise. *Kindling the Native Spirit*. Hay House, 2015.

Macartney, Mac. *The Children's Fire: Heart Song of a People*. Practical Inspiration Publishing, 2018.

Macy, Joanna and Brown, Molly. *Coming Back to Life*. New Society Publishers, 2014.

Minmia. *Under the Quandong Tree*. Quandong Dreaming Publishing, 2017.

Neale, Linda. *The Power of Ceremony, Restoring the Sacred in Our Selves, Our Families, Our Communities*. Eagle Spirit Press, 2011.

O'Donohue, John. *To Bless the Space Between Us.* Convergent Books, 2008.

Patrice Somé, Malidoma. *Ritual: Power, Healing, and Community.* Penguin, 1997.

Pfeiffer, Bill. *Wild Earth, Wild Soul.* Moon Books, 2013.

Pinkola Estes, Clarissa, *Women Who Run With Wolves.* Rider, 1992.

Plotkin, Bill. *Soulcraft, Crossing into the Mysteries of Nature and Psyche.* New World Library, 2003.

Pretchel, Martin. *Long Life, Honey in the Heart: A Story of Initiation and Eloquence from the Shores of a Mayan Lake.* Jeremy P Tarcher, 1999.

Ramsay, Jay. *Alchemy, The Art of Transformation.* Thorsons, 1997.

Ronnberg, Ami and Martin, Kathleen (editors). *The Book of Symbols: Reflections on Archetypal Images.* Taschen, 2010.

Schrader, Claire (editor). *Ritual Theatre, The Power of Dramatic Ritual in Personal Development, Groups and Clinical Practice.* Jessica Kingsley Publishers, 2012.

Simmons, Laurey. *The Inner Beauty Bible.* Thorsons, 2017.

Starhawk and Baker, Diane and Hill, Anne. *Circle Round, Raising Children in the Goddess Traditions.* Bantam Books, 2000.

Turner, Toko-pa. *Belonging: Remembering Ourselves Home.* Her Own Room Press, 2017.

Turner, Victor (editor). *The Ritual Process: Structure and Anti-Structure.* Cornell University, 1977.

Williams, Mike. *The Shaman's Spirit: Discovering the Wisdom of Nature, Power Animals, Sacred Places and Rituals.* London: Watkins, 2013.

Zweig, Connie and Wolf, Steve. *Romancing the Shadow.* Ballantine Books, 1997.

Tree-planting

Treesisters: https://treesisters.org/give

World Land Trust: https://www.worldlandtrust.org/donate/

Trees for Life (Scotland): https://treesforlife.org.uk/product/donate/

Pilgrimage

British Pilgrimage Trust: https://britishpilgrimage.org/

English Heritage: https://www.english-heritage.org.uk/pilgrimage

Meditation retreat centres

Gaia House: https://gaiahouse.co.uk/

The Barn Retreat: https://www.sharphamtrust.org/mindfulness-retreats/the-barn-retreat

Organisations

Embercombe: https://embercombe.org/

WildWise: https://wildwise.co.uk/

Ritual tools & herbs

Stag & Seer: https://www.stagseer.com/

Jade Moon: https://www.earthsmokebonesong.co.uk/online-store

Starchild: https://starchild.co.uk/

Music

Carolyn Hillier: https://www.seventhwavemusic.co.uk/instruments/the-antlered-drum/

Dorrie Joy: https://www.dorriejoy.co.uk/workshops

Drumming track for journeying: Sandra Ingerman 'Soul Journeys, Music for Shamanic Practice', Sounds True, August 2010.

Acknowledgements

I offer my deepest gratitude to all beings, seen and unseen, who supported the dreaming, creating and birth of this book. With special mention to the spirit of the land I live with in Bruton, Grandmama Chestnut Tree and the River Brue, for holding me on this journey and bringing forth such wild inspiration and grounding. I thank my ancestor Ivy and Ancient Grandmothers for helping me remember these old ways of honouring the sacred, and dear Brighid for calling me to attend to this flame and for keeping the spring bubbling with life.

This book was brought to life by the exquisite illustrations of Luisa Rivera, to whom I am forever grateful for agreeing to collaborate with me, and for all the beauty and colour she gifts to the world. I thank my editor Gaynor Sermon for her encouragement and steady presence throughout, and all those at Laurence King Publishing who have given their time and energy to this book. Thank you to my agent Valeria Huerta for seeing the potential in me, and to the magical Kelly Thompson for midwifing the seed of an idea into a workable garden. With gratitude to Gary Hawke for the ways he encouraged me to look beyond the surface of things and explore more deeply the realms of ritual, creativity and words.

In giving thanks, I remember and praise all those teachers who have enriched my life, including all the tree, plant, mushroom and animal guides who have blessed my way. I thank all wisdom-keepers in all forms who have protected our ancient, indigenous knowledge and carried the seeds of hope in their hearts. I offer my gratitude to all the people I have worked with over the years, who have supported me in honing my craft and provided such juicy material to explore the potential of ritual with.

My greatest teacher and favourite companion, my son and songbird Wren – thank you for being my eternal source of inspiration and for filling our home with such love and laughter. I am grateful to my family for creating such a strong foundation for me to grow from, for all their care and support, and to my beautiful friends who help me feed the flame and keep dancing and whose unwavering encouragement expanded my capacity to write from my heart. Thank you.

I am overflowing with gratitude for all trees from whom this book is made, and to all my tree kin for the breath of life that courses through its pages. And I thank you dear reader, for picking up this book and looking within. Bless you.

About the author

Isla Macleod is a ritual designer with over a decade of experience of ritual practice, drawing inspiration from indigenous traditions and the natural world. As a trained shamanic healer and celebrant she has presided over a wide range of ceremonies, blessings and seasonal celebrations, and creates bespoke workshops and retreats that offer respite for those seeking connection and meaning. Isla has a particular interest in crafting, herbalism, music and ecology, and through her work seeks to encourage us to re-connect with nature and discover the sacred in the everyday in order to live intentionally and creatively. She lives in the beautiful vales of Somerset in south west England with her son, Wren.

islamacleod.com
www.instagram.com/islajmacleod/